THE
SECOND
INCARNATION

THE SECOND INCARNATION

Empowering the Church
for the 21st Century

DR. RANDALL J. HARRIS
DR. RUBEL SHELLY

HOWARD
PUBLISHING CO.
3117 North 7th Street
West Monroe, LA 71291

The purpose of Howard Publishing is threefold:

- **Instructing** believers toward a deeper faith in Jesus Christ
- **Inspiring** holiness in the lives of believers
- **Instilling** hope in the hearts of struggling people everywhere

Because he's coming again

Howard Publishing Co., Inc.
3117 North 7th Street, West Monroe, LA 71291-2227

The Second Incarnation
© 1992 by Howard Publishing
All rights reserved. First Printing 1992
Second Impression 1995
Printed in the United States of America

Cover design by LinDee Loveland

ISBN: 1-878990-21-7

DEDICATION

To our parents:

James and Lucille Shelly

and

Cecil and Joanna Harris

CONTENTS

Fundamental Relations

Ecclesiology and Eschatology

PREFACE

This book originated in an early morning Bible study. The two of us, along with Jim Samuel, were meeting on a weekly basis to study Scripture and reflect on theological readings. After reading a book we thought fell short of its possibilities because of an impoverished ecclesiology, someone in the group said, "Someone needs to push us to rethink the subject of the church. It is the only corrective to this sort of mistake."

We began talking about the parameters of a biblical doctrine of the church. We spoke about the demands of the 21st century that could be met only with such a clarified ecclesiology. What form would it take? How could it be communicated? What impact might it have?

The possibility of serious research that could lead to a book began to emerge from our discussions. As we read and talked, specifics began to come into view. Then Jim Samuel moved from Nashville and left the project with us, encouraging that it be carried through.

We taught a six-month class for the Woodmont Hills church in which we first shared some of our embryonic ideas. The formulation of the entire project around the Pauline metaphor of the church as body of Christ came clear for us. The concept of the church as a "second incarnation" both intrigued and challenged class participants. Valuable feedback from the class forced us to clarify and delineate our fundamental ideas.

Since that time, we have had occasion to share—sometimes together and sometimes separately—that early material. It has sparked healthy discussion. It has brought about wholesome changes in attitude among people disillusioned with the church. It has stimulated the recasting of church programs and outreach.

As ideas became notes became chapter plans became rough drafts, the requests for the material in permanent form increased. We hope this book will not only satisfy those pleas but result in widespread dialogue about a viable theology of the church. For those who appreciate what we offer, we caution that these ideas are put forth as suggestive rather than final. For our detractors, we offer the same reply as our only defense.

Our prayer is that God will bless this book to serve its purpose of exciting the sort of study that has proved so helpful to us. If others' conclusions differ from ours, we are satisfied to have called them to the task of pondering such an important theme.

RUBEL SHELLY
RANDALL J. HARRIS

INTRODUCTION

Who Needs Ecclesiology?

This work is an exercise in basic *ecclesiology*, which is the study of the doctrine of the church. It does not intend to work at the level (or length) of the books on the church by Hans Kung or Jurgen Moltmann, which, though penetrating in their insights, tend to be unduly intimidating to lay persons. We choose rather to write for those thoughtful church members we have found scattered everywhere who are looking for a clearer and deeper vision of the church, worthy of their life-commitment.

While we come from a particular religious tradition, we hope to say something helpful to all those who share with us the basic convictions of the deity and lordship of Jesus, the inspiration and authority of Scripture, and the call to Christian community.

But, with all the pressing needs in our world, who needs ecclesiology? Before asking the reader to take this book seriously, we feel a need to answer this question. In doing so, we both attempt to justify our efforts at writing and your venture in reading. *The 21st-century church needs ecclesiology for a variety of reasons.*

First, we need ecclesiology because we are enmeshed in an ever-changing world. Doctrine works between the two poles of faithfulness to Scripture and relevance to the present age. The task of being the church for *our age* must be rethought continually. Simply reciting verses from the Bible is no guarantee that a viable modern community of faith will be developed. We need a faith for *today* and a concept of the church to match it. So ecclesiology must be a continuing task, always responding to the newness of the world in which we live, constantly rethinking what it means to be a church that keeps us from getting stagnant.

Second, we need ecclesiology to insure that we do not lose our true calling in the midst of institutional activity. Many church members find themselves in a flurry of activity, constantly running from one church program to another. Many of these works are undoubtedly noble, but we must take care lest we find ourselves maintaining an institution rather than advancing the kingdom of God. The church ought always to pursue a "kingdom agenda" in the world, but the kingdom of God can never be contained fully in any human enterprise. If we become preoccupied with maintaining our institutional structures—or, worse still, our denominational identities and traditions—we may frustrate heaven's intention to use the church as its mechanism for penetrating history with the kingdom of God.

There is an old story about a group of orange pickers who decided to come together to discuss how they might do their job more efficiently. They soon were involved in writing manuals on orange picking and having orange-picking seminars and writing songs to encourage orange picking. They even had national conventions dedicated to the worthy profession of picking oranges. Unfortunately, while all this was going on, no one was picking oranges. The fruit died and rotted on the trees.

We must all pause now and again to be sure that those matters which gave rise to the church in the first place are still at the heart of what we say and do. It is the way we chart our course for the future.

Third, we need ecclesiology to humble us. When we capture a vision of the church as God intended it, we are always driven to see our own inability to fulfill that vision. It will not do to take undue pride in the achievements of any particular congregation or religious tradition. When we understand all that the church ought to be, the only response must be "Woe is me! I dwell in the midst of a people of unclean lips." This leads, of course, not to despair but to humble, hopeful faith. Salvation is finally not a product of human achievement but of divine grace. We cannot hear this too often.

And why do we propose a theology for the *21st-century* church? It is certainly not that we think we have the remainder of a decade to get clearer in our thinking about and holier in our pursuit of the kingdom. To the contrary, we are not under the delusion that we are preparing for a new reality that will be ushered in with the chronological entry into a new century and millennium. We believe we have already entered it!

We would echo Peter Drucker's thesis that "the 'next century' is already here, indeed we are well advanced into it."[1] The political, economic, and social landscapes of our world have changed. Continuing to operate on old assumptions about the role of government will guarantee a politician's failure: witness the fate of Central and Eastern European leaders. Continuing to argue the old economic strategies will assure disaster: the current confusion in both East and West proves as much. Continuing the workings of business, education, and other social functions on the old models we have used cannot succeed: we still have not realized this truism widely enough to make needed changes.

And it is no different with the functioning of the church. The world we are forced to live in, commissioned to serve, and called to evangelize is described above as having changed its landscape. How, then, can we be so naive to think that addressing the issues of a time now past will communicate divine reality to our time? For that matter, can we assure ourselves that we were ever as effective in this task as we should have been?

We have not intended to speak to every topic connected with ecclesiology but to reexamine the foundations upon which all such efforts must be built. If we open the door for others to explore fruitful areas we have omitted, we can only be grateful for stimulating their work. When others do better work with the topics we have raised, we will rejoice

---

1. Peter Drucker, *The New Realities* (New York: Harper & Row, Publishers, 1989), p. ix.

and learn from them rather than take offense. If someone feels compelled to correct something here, we will attempt to listen to the objection raised. Only the Word of God is normative. This book is another in a series of flawed attempts by all-too-fallible disciples to understand its meaning for the life of the church.

From the Table of Contents, our readers may discern an intended flow of the book's material. First, we address the issue of change for the church in two ways. Is there either the need or theological warrant for ongoing change in the church? Our answer is affirmative to both elements of this question. But how shall we avoid change that is destructive of God's purpose for the church? A chapter on Scripture and its role for the life of the church is included at this point. The biblical data must anchor the church during its seasons of challenge and response over the centuries. To look at it another way, Chapter One focuses on an observed need for change and advances some preliminary theological insights about perpetual divine renewal as God's will for his people. Then Chapter Two pursues the issue of grounding theology firmly in Scripture so that the church answers to the Spirit of God rather than to the spirit of the age. We reject the thesis that "the world sets the church's agenda"; we affirm that God has set the church's agenda via revelation. When the church pursues its divinely established mission, it will avoid the stagnation and irrelevance that too often afflict us.

Second, we move directly to offer a view of the church that arises from the position taken on

Scripture in Chapter Two. Working from the premise that the church reflects the glory of the triune God, we offer something of a trinitarian conception of the identity, nature, and community of the unique society known as the church. Chapter Three explores the Pauline metaphor of the church as Christ's spiritual body; Chapter Four attempts to give focus to the complex relationships between a time-bounded people and the eternal kingdom of God; Chapter Five acknowledges the Holy Spirit as the internal dynamic of the community of faith we call the church. Just as the three persons of the Godhead are ultimately inseparable, so are these three issues inseparable in the practical outworkings of the ecclesiology proposed in this book.

Third, we face the flesh-and-blood implications of our ecclesiology for individual congregations. If our readers detect an uneasy and sometimes unclear delineation between church-as-intended and church-as-is in the first section of the volume, we confess to its presence. What is more, we know of no way to eliminate the inherent tension between the two. With a view of the church as God's people still in the process of becoming, the two will not be synonymous until Christ's return. For readers whose most urgent concern is for the practical ramifications of this sort of thinking about the church, however, the question of applicability will haunt him or her constantly. What does this view of the church mean in terms of worship? How does it relate to evangelism? Chapters Six through Nine grapple with these and related matters.

Finally, we propose an ecclesiology that is oriented more toward the future than the past for its ultimate significance in God's eternal purpose. The church will not arrive at its goal within historical events. Its Christological character, argued for in this book's opening chapters and traced through its ongoing routines in intervening chapters, will come to full and final form only at the return of Jesus. Thus the church waits for "his appearing and kingdom." In the meanwhile, the body bears witness to its head in baptism and the Lord's Supper (Chapter Ten) as "symbols of the promise." Chapter Eleven argues that the end of time brings about the realization of all God ever intended the church to be.

This work is ultimately a testimony to our love for the church. It seeks to be a positive contribution to the only project worthy of a lifetime's devotion—not the defending of a denominational stance or sectarian creed or human institution—but becoming "the fullness of him who fills everything in every way."

A New Doctrine of the Church?

Possibilities and Limitations

CHAPTER ONE

The Freedom to Change

An essential feature of the God of Judeo-Christian theism is *immutability*. The term affirms that God's nature is not subject to change. "I the Lord do not change" (Mal. 3:6; cf. Heb. 1:12).

Furthermore, the essential doctrines of the Christian faith have been "once for all entrusted to the saints" (Jude 3). We have neither the right nor the need to change the gospel affirmations about Jesus and salvation in him alone.

The church, however, is different. It does not possess the immutability of divine personality. Nor does it have the unalterable quality of propositional truth. The church is a *divine-human enterprise* which, though called into being by God's will, cannot escape the imperfections of its membership. It is a *dynamic organism* that both reflects and challenges its environment. It is a *living body* that alternately thrives and declines. The church does change. Moreover, it needs to change.

3

Divine Self-Disclosure

God has made himself known through the general revelation of himself in creation (Rom. 1:20; cf. Psa. 19:1) and through the specific revelation of himself and his will through words (2 Pet. 1:20-21). This process of self-disclosure to his human creatures reached its crescendo in the Incarnation of the Son. "The Word became flesh and lived for a while among us," proclaimed John. "We have seen his glory, the glory of the one and only Son, who came from the Father, full of grace and truth" (John 1:14). The opening lines of Hebrews affirm: "In the past God spoke to our forefathers through the prophets at many times and in various ways, but in these last days he has spoken to us by his Son, whom he appointed heir of all things, and through whom he made the universe. The Son is the radiance of God's glory and the exact representation of his being" (Heb. 1:1-4). But, while God's revelation of himself reached its zenith in the Incarnate Word, it continues through the church. As the spiritual body of Christ visible in local congregations, the church perpetuates, with the aid of the Holy Spirit, the process of incarnation. Jesus remains incarnate in his church.

What the church *is* (i.e., God's second incarnation) and what the church *does* (i.e., its daily life) will always be incongruous. Just as the thoughtful Christian knows that his standing (i.e., imputed righteousness) is far above his performance (i.e., lived righteousness), the reflective church acknowledges a status superior to its conduct. This disparity is not emphasized here for the sake of rebuke or

with a goal of disheartening anyone. To the contrary, it is intended to encourage the dejected soul
who is weighed down with a dual sense of personal
inadequacy and of the church's failings.

A fictional character once answered a critic of
the church with these words:

> The real church . . . is nothing less than the
> laboratory of the new community of mankind
> which God's love through Christ keeps trying
> to shape humanity into. It is nothing less
> than the laboratory of a God-created commu-
> nity, called into this world by Him and depen-
> ding on Him for all its life and energy. . . .
> It's as if with each generation, right in the
> teeth of whatever's threatening humanity the
> worst, the Master Conductor is calling to-
> gether another ragtag orchestra of amateur
> musicians and asking us to play music that's
> so great we can't quite play it! Yet, in the very
> trying and for all the bungling, for all the dis-
> cordant sound of our efforts, some things get
> done for God in our time. Some things get
> done for Christ that, without the church,
> wouldn't get done.[1]

Isn't that a wonderful thought with which to balance cynicism and skepticism about the church?
Yet we seek a paradigm for imitation in trying to
be the church. We want a pattern to follow. We long
for a model to copy.

---

1. Frederick B. Speakman, *God and Jack Wilson* (Old Tappan, NJ:
Fleming H. Revell Co., 1965), pp. 54, 56.

For the individual believer, Christ's perfect example remains the benchmark for his or her life. For the corporate body of Christ, there is no historical prototype of the church for duplication. The kingdom of God is yet to come in its ultimate form. In all its instantiations, the church has been (and is) flawed. It is not a fixed, static institution. It has no once-for-all form. It is a body growing and forming. Its vision is fundamentally eschatological, thus looking forward rather than backward for its hope. In devotion to the immutable God and with fidelity to its once-for-all truth articulated in Scripture and personified in Christ, the church is a process. It is always happening as little enclaves of the kingdom of heaven break into human experience.

The first church was the Jerusalem church. We tend to point back to it and advocate using that church as a "pattern" for our imitation. Shall we imitate Ananias and Sapphira in their attempted deception of the church's leaders? Shall we imitate that church's neglect of its needy widows? Or the grumbling and discord that neglect produced? Shall we imitate its racial exclusiveness and the resulting lack of evangelistic activity? That church needed to change.

Even if a perfect church existed, faithfulness would demand that we look beyond it to keep our focus on the person of Jesus. Attempting to be Christ's *spiritual* body, we can orient all our teaching, ministries, and corporate life to his example. A given church needs to change whenever it can do something to move closer to his likeness. It needs to remain open to renewal. The last thing it can afford is inflexibility and defiance toward change.

Unlike our perfect God or his inscripturated Word, the church is *not* immutable. It has no once-for-all complexion. Yet our habit is to foster obstinacy when great versatility and resilience are needed. Through the centuries, attempts to "reproduce the New Testament church" have repeatedly let the noble idea of faithfulness degenerate into closed-minded partisanship, have understood soundness to signify hard-line traditionalism, and have prostituted the ministry of teaching into authoritarian indoctrination. The result has been twofold: (1) leadership that took the form of domineering supervision and (2) a discipline that amounted to ruthless castigation and/or banishment for those who could not abide such a ponderous system.

Among Jews or Gentiles, blacks or whites, Europeans or Americans, white-collar professionals or blue-collar employees, differences of corporate temperament, musical taste, communication style, etc. are inevitable. The unvarying God who called the church into being and the stipulated doctrinal base upon which it rests cannot be tampered with or replaced. But the culture-based methods used to model and present the gospel must vary according to the needs of the people who are asked to hear it.

The Church's Self-Analysis

Some churches are daring to analyze themselves. They are asking interesting questions such as: What are the distinctive marks of this juncture in history? What challenges to the gospel are implicit in our culture? What openings for the gospel are possible in this culture? What are the concerns of this generation? How does the Christian religion address those concerns intelligibly? How can we display the gospel's unique message most effectively? What do we need to challenge and try to change in our culture? What is there about us that needs to change so we can be God's instrument to bless our culture?

Perceptive questions such as these have led to changes in some churches. The time and nature of church assemblies have been altered. Educational programs have been adapted. Local church ministries have been revamped to meet special community needs and interests. Time-honored traditions about how to accomplish certain ends have been replaced with creative innovations. The church's approach to certain people has been rethought.

Some churches no longer own and maintain expensive buildings; others invest staggering amounts of money into multi-purpose facilities. Either approach may be justifiable in the face of a particular need.

Some churches still have successful and fruitful Vacation Bible School programs in the summer; others have either abandoned these programs altogether or have transformed them into one-day, circus-type events to introduce community children to the church. Either approach can be justified in light of a particular setting.

There are churches that open the doors of their buildings to non-religious community groups such as Alcoholics Anonymous, while others structure programs to help chemically dependent persons that are more distinctively tied to Christian doctrine and lifestyle. Either approach can be appropriate.

These changes frighten some people. They may appear "secular" rather than "churchy." But fear among some who may be too wedded to traditional understandings and methods must not be permitted to hinder needed change. Change can be both desirable and spiritual.

A preacher in a dark suit who quotes dozens of lengthy passages from the Bible may be doing a wonderful work. In some settings we can imagine, he would be the best teacher for the group. But what about a dramatic presentation by 15 men and women that communicates the will of God? Or a quartet? Or a preacher who trades his dark suit for blue jeans and a sweatshirt? These things we view as "changes" are the norm in many foreign mission settings.

"One size fits all" may be a neat idea for cheap socks. It probably isn't such a good idea for the worship assemblies, outreach programs, or educational ministries of the church.

Some attempts at change will not work. Some will be counter-productive. They will need to be scrapped or revised. Even so, these "unsuccessful" attempts have the virtue of being efforts made to do God's will. Their value lies in creating an atmosphere of openness and flexibility. Only such deeds as have no human involvement at any level can be vouchsafed perfect in advance of their execution.

Some changed methodologies *will* work. Their worth to the task of making the church into a zone of spiritual integrity in a fallen and broken world will be unmistakable. They can be studied, imitated, and adapted to other situations.

We must not be guilty of trying to limit God to the deep ruts we have worn. Jesus Christ will not be confined to our traditions and limitations today any more than he would be bound to those he encountered in the first century.

We are not writing this book as an appeal for or a defense of *faddishness*. Moving with every trendy, chic idea that comes down the pike is foolishness. Indeed, some core essentials are unalterable, permanent, and fixed. These give continuity and durability to the church. They have enabled this imperfect entity known as the church to exist through two millennia. With all its divisions, heresies, and self-promoting personalities, the gates of Hades have not yet prevailed against it. The fixed things to which the church is linked (i.e., God and Scripture) have kept it from destruction.

A God of Newness

The fact remains, however, that the God of the Bible is always a God of new things. Through the Old Testament prophets, he promised a new name (Isa. 62:2), a new covenant (Jer. 31:31), a new spirit (Ezek. 11:19), and a new heart (Ezek. 36:26). When Jesus came, all these new things moved from promise to reality. They were not fads. They were genuinely new things. They created an atmosphere of freshness and exhilaration.

Jesus said it would be dangerous to try to contain the new, fermenting wine of the gospel of the kingdom of God in the old wineskins of religious tradition. "No one pours new wine into old wineskins," he said. "If he does, the new wine will burst the skins, the wine will run out and the wineskins will be ruined. No, new wine must be poured into new wineskins" (Luke 5:37-38).

Change and newness did not end with his arrival. *The wine is still fermenting.* Tired forms will not work with an exuberant message. The deep ruts of customary practice are not adequate to be a highway of holiness. The gospel he left to inform and empower his church is "a new and living way" (Heb. 10:20).

The abiding challenge to the people of God is to distinguish the *wine* from the *wineskins*, the essential from the discretionary. We must not equate the refreshing gospel with vestiges of an outmoded tradition. The wineskins are supposed to carry and bequeath the wine to thirsty souls. But stretched, worn, and outdated wineskins become problems in themselves. The gospel continues to ferment, however, and bursts them.

The wine is the bubbling, churning gospel. It is the ever-arriving-yet-never-fully-realized-on-Earth kingdom of God. It is the powerful presence of the Spirit of God among believers. The wineskins are the points of contact between the wine and culture. They are the forms and programs we maintain, the organizations and institutions, or the patterns and procedures.

The alternative to rigidity and destruction is constant renewal. Individual believers need ongoing invigoration from the Spirit of God. So do whole churches. We must offer ourselves as fresh, flexible wineskins to Christ daily. The options to change, adjustment, and newness in our forms and institutions are limited.

One possibility is to opt for the old wine of religious legalism as an alternative to the ever-new wine of the gospel. We can embrace and affirm only the comfortable and familiar. There will be no fermentation, no stretching, no joy.

A second alternative might involve an attempt to fill the old forms and institutions with new wine. The fermentation will begin, and the process will create unbearable tension. The skins will eventually break, spilling the wine.

We reject both of these strategies. Both are dead ends for something so dynamic as the gospel of the kingdom of heaven. God surely calls his people to a higher and nobler task than stubborn inflexibility. It is beyond our ability to imagine the great God of Scripture as bound to a single time or culture, as restricted to our limited personal understandings or sectarian fellowships.

In writing this book, we are not claiming to know all the changes that need to be made in today's church. Much less do we know how to make them or what the finished product in a given situation should look like. We only know that for us the alternative to change is unacceptable, destructive, and fatal.

- We must refocus our identity in terms of Jesus as the head of a living, growing, changing spiritual body as an alternative to the static institutional model most seem to have.
- The tired, uninspiring event called worship in our churches must give way to an exhilarating experience of God that simultaneously exhibits and nurtures life in the worshippers.
- The life of the church must be less a series of promotions and programs and more a loving atmosphere for sin-confessing, faith-sharing, support-giving believers.
- The church must take holiness, discipline, and piety seriously enough that its life as the body of Christ will convince an unbelieving world of the reality of Jesus and its need for salvation in him.
- We must understand our mission to the world on the model of salt and light—serving it, challenging it, exhibiting Jesus to it—rather than retreating from it into the insulated fortress of smug religiosity.

Don't feel threatened by the prospect. Be excited about it and allow yourself to be open to renewal. Ask God to make you a receptive, yielded vessel. Pray for the wisdom to distinguish the primary wine from the secondary wineskins, the essential from the non-essential.

Realist that he was, Jesus knew that most people would prefer the taste of old wine over new. "And no one after drinking old wine wants the new, for he says, 'The old is better'" (Luke 5:39). The old is familiar and comfortable. It makes no demands, produces no tension, and causes no discomfort.

Christ's challenge to us is to abandon comfort and security for the sake of change and improvement. Moving beyond fear of the gospel's new wine, then, each of us can decide to be an eager instrument of God's purpose to renew his church on the brink of the 21st century. Without renewal, we will become increasingly irrelevant to God's purpose in the world and will be broken, spilling and wasting the precious wine of the gospel. Without renewal, we will have diminished value, either to the purposes of a holy God or to the needs of a lost world.

The first test of any proposed change in our method of doing God's work must always be: *Does it correspond to the person, teaching, and lifestyle of Jesus of Nazareth as revealed in the New Testament?* Other tests are: Does it get a favorable hearing for the Word of God? Does it communicate effectively? Does it make a practical difference in the lives of people? Does it affect people the way Jesus' ministry affected them?

If the response to the first question is "No"— even if the ringing affirmation to the remainder is "Yes"—the proposed change is unjustified. But whenever the answer to the first question is "Yes" and to the others is "No," something needs to change.

Conclusion

As we are propelled into a new century, we must be honest enough to ask ourselves whether our theology of the church is adequate for this age. The sad truth may be that some fellowships and traditions are already so outdated and irrelevant that they cannot catch up. We hope the church will be aggressive enough to face the 21st century with a resourcefulness equal to the challenges before us and worthy of the gospel entrusted to us. And our hope is that this book will make a contribution to both those ends.

To use Jack Wilson's words again, God is still calling together ragtag orchestras of amateur musicians to play music so great we "can't quite play it." For all our bungling, however, some things are getting done for Christ that wouldn't get done otherwise. Oh, that we could play it more beautifully and offer it as a sweeter sound to our Master Conductor! Oh, that we could make it more suitable as a testimony to the world of his salvific genius!

Because we believe in a living and powerful God who acts among and through his people, we refuse to believe that he cannot rouse us from our spiritual lethargy and embolden our witness to the Lord Jesus Christ. "Now to him who is able to do immeasurably more than all we ask or imagine, according to his power that is at work within us, to him be glory in the church and in Christ Jesus throughout all generations, for ever and ever? Amen" (Eph. 3:20-21).

CHAPTER TWO

Scripture:
The Anchor of the Church

The church must change to fulfill its divine purpose. But what is to prevent the church from adopting faddish excesses or simply drifting along on the currents of popular culture? What will save the church from such extreme accommodation to culture that she loses any distinctive message? While the church must be willing to change and adapt, it also must be anchored by something trans-cultural to prevent it from being lost in the world and worldliness. We believe that anchor point is Holy Scripture, and the explication of this thesis will occupy our attention in this chapter.

Taking the Bible into hand for reading and interpretation is both essential and humbling. Thus we must go to the task with both eagerness and caution.

Opposite the site of ancient Luxor, one finds the 62 known tombs of the Valley of the Kings. Over a millennium before the birth of Christ, the

Egyptians buried their mummies there. Modern visitors go to the location by the hundreds of thousands each year. As the tourists go through the tombs and marvel at the burial chambers, they are doing unintended but permanent harm to their contents.

Small black specks and blotches now mar the tomb walls. These blemishes are rapidly multiplying bacteria, long dormant in the paint itself but now activated by rising humidity imported by curious visitors. Sweat and breath from the visitors to King Tut's tomb on any given day nourish the bacteria and produce damage to the painted walls. Just six people breathing inside that single-chambered tomb for one hour can raise the humidity by five percent.

The people who visit these places surely mean no harm to the treasured tombs. By their very presence, however, they contribute to their degeneration. They are damaging something they value by their mere presence.

Our view is that something of the same nature is likely to happen when we enter the sacred realm of divine revelation. Revelation from God's mind to our minds does occur through the Bible, and we can understand the divine will adequately—though neither exhaustively nor incorrigibly—by reading it. And we can be saved by the knowledge of the gospel that has been mediated to us through the written Word of God. The fact remains, though, that our methods of inquiry and analysis are human rather than divine, fallible rather than flawless.

There is a *single* God-breathed revelation of heaven to humankind. It is preserved for us in the 66 books of our canonical Bible. It is divine and authoritative. But there is *no* infallible method for interpreting Scripture. There is no heaven-given system of Bible study. And every method ever offered for handling the Bible responsibly—including the one to be outlined in this chapter—is human and fallible.

An admission of this sort is not placed at the front of the chapter to produce discouragement. It is an appeal for humility. It is meant to call for willingness to subject one's findings to the scrutiny of others. And it is a warning against our human tendency to want to supplant the Lord Jesus Christ as judge of all.

Most of us, as we come to Scripture, bring to our reading the heritage of a particular religious tradition. Many of us have deep personal ties and commitments to such traditions. It is, of course, inevitable that such experiences will have an impact on our interpretation of Scripture. We are under no illusion that our reading of Scripture is pure while everyone else's is prejudiced. It is not our purpose to attempt to bludgeon everyone into conformity with our views. But we do believe that every religious tradition must be self-critical. We hope that the members of a wide variety of Christian heritages will answer the challenge to rethink the theological foundations of the living church. If this talk is entered seriously and prayerfully, all of us will find matters that need to be brought into greater conformity with the Living Lord.

Thus warned about the seriousness of the task at hand and put on guard against sinful arrogance, we must face the issue of how church and Scripture relate. Specifically, we must seek for a sense in which the Bible "anchors" the church. We must also look for a set of workable principles that can guide us in conducting responsible inquiries into the meaning of the sacred text.

Ecclesiology and the Bible

If the question *"What should the modern church be like?"* were put to members of evangelical churches, someone would surely reply, "The church today should be like the first-century church we read about in the New Testament." But is it really so simple? An imaginary dialogue can illustrate the problem.

"If the church today should be like the one we read about in the New Testament, do you mean we should have open fornication and abuses of the Lord's Supper like in Corinth?"

"Of course not," comes the reply. "We shouldn't imitate the sins and weaknesses of the early church, but the divine *pattern* set out there."

"Oh, I see. Then we should have charismatic worship services that include tongue-speaking— with an interpreter, of course—like some early churches did?"

"No, no, no! Everyone knows that has been done away with. It's alright to give up things like that, but we mustn't *add* anything new."

"Then I guess you'll want to tear the New Testaments out of all our Bibles, since the earliest church had only the Old Testament?"

"Don't be silly. We must have our New Testaments to be good Christians. I just mean we should imitate the life and worship of early Christians as revealed in the New Testament except for miraculous spiritual gifts."

"So we must practice the holy kiss, women wearing veils, and the financial collectivism of the early Jerusalem church today?"

"No, those are cultural matters. What I mean is . . . I don't really know what I mean."

Perhaps this imaginary but quite believable conversation indicates that the answer to our question (i.e., "What should the modern church be like?") is not quite so simple as we sometimes think or pretend. So we are forced to ask again: How do we move responsibly from ancient Scripture to the 21st-century world?

Our task in this segment of the study is to try to understand the role of Scripture in developing a vision for the modern church. This will involve us in a discussion of *hermeneutics*, which is the technical term for the study of the principles of interpretation. To understand the crucial place of Scripture for developing a modern ecclesiology, we must answer these questions: (1) What is the nature of Scripture? (2) How do I get at the intended meaning of the text? (3) How do I apply the text to the contemporary situation of the 21st-century church?

The Nature of Scripture

To understand the nature of Scripture with any degree of sufficiency, we must understand in what sense the Bible is *the Word of God* and in what sense it is *a word of man.* A clear concept of the dual nature of Scripture is crucial to all that follows.

We believe Scripture to be the Word of God, the God who created us and who is unchanging in his nature. Given God's eternal faithfulness to his own identity, his word is eternally binding and always relevant. Scripture can never be ignored, nor can we outgrow it. It is the primary source of our knowledge of God today. Thus we affirm without hesitation such classic texts as 2 Timothy 3:16-17 ("All Scripture is God-breathed") and 2 Peter 1:21 ("For prophecy never had its origin in the will of man, but men spoke from God as they were carried along by the Holy Spirit").

It is not our purpose in this book to present Christian apologetics, so no effort will be made here to prove the inspiration of the Bible. Several books are available that take on this task.[1] But we must stress that for us the Bible is not just history, not merely the presentation of the reflections of great men of faith, and not simply sage spiritual advice; it is *revelation from God.*

As we reflect on a doctrine of the church for our age, we do not feel free either to ignore Scripture or even to view it as theological counsel that one may accept or reject. It is, rather, God's authoritative disclosure of his will for us. A primary goal of this book is to be faithful to the truth revealed in Scripture. For us, the question is not *whether* the Bible speaks authoritatively for Christians, for we do not see how this can be otherwise. The question,

---

1. See, for example, Rubel Shelly, *Prepare to Answer: A Defense of the Christian Faith* (Grand Rapids: Baker Book House, 1990).

rather, is *how to understand* the Word of God for our time.

But to see Scripture as the Word of God does not fully comprehend the nature of the Bible. It is also *a word of man*. If God is going to communicate with human beings, it cannot be in God-talk (whatever that may be) but must be in human language. So the Bible comes to us in the midst of a particular human culture, among particular historical events, and in a particular human language. If God wishes to speak to man, how could it be otherwise?

While accepting Peter's statement that "no prophecy of Scripture came about by the prophet's own interpretation" (2 Pet. 1:20), it is nevertheless still true that the Spirit-guided words of the prophets were delivered in space and time, in words of ordinary human vocabulary, within the context of distinctive historical events, and in the midst of identifiable human cultures.

If God chooses to speak to human beings, whatever pure and unhindered method of communication is used within the Godhead must be abandoned for the sake of human language. The Bible is the result of that process. It is the Word of God as delivered to us through the medium of human language. Changeless divine truth is thus enmeshed in the ever-changing vehicle of human language. Perfect and eternal wisdom is wrapped up in the inferior medium of historical disclosure.

Calvin once referred to the Bible as "God's baby talk." By such a term, he meant no disrespect for Scripture and was not denying its truthfulness. He was simply struggling to communicate the point we are making here. For God to communicate with finite beings in our sinful state, he had to work at a very minimal-for-him level that nevertheless constitutes still a greater-than-us quality of disclosure.

Human culture differs from age to age and from society to society. If God had chosen to reveal himself at a different time and in a different culture, he surely would have presented the eternal message in the cultural and linguistic trappings of *that* time and place.

We must be clear about this if we are to read Scripture responsibly. Failing to see the human side of the revelation process, we may find ourselves reproducing first-century culture rather than preserving the message embedded therein.

Deriving the Meaning of Scripture

Understanding the dual nature of Scripture is crucial to answering our second question about the intended meaning of the text. The process of finding the intended meaning of a biblical text is called *exegesis*, which basically means getting out of a text what is really there. Exegesis has essentially two steps.

First, there is *historical analysis*. This is an attempt to understand the culture and history of whatever text one is studying. Since the Bible comes from ancient times and distant places, we do this kind of research to understand the customs, language, forms, and analogies used in Scripture to convey the will of God.

To illustrate our point, consider that 1 Corinthians 11:1-16 preserves a detailed discussion about whether women should wear a veil when they speak in church. Without some understanding of the meaning of veils in that particular culture (something completely foreign to modern Americans), it is impossible to read this passage in a meaningful way. Historical study is intended to shed light on such problems.

The fact that Scripture comes in the midst of human history and culture makes this necessary. Anyone who has read Shakespeare's historical plays knows that a certain amount of effort directed at comprehending the historical setting is necessary for the fullest understanding of the play. The same is true in reading the Bible. The Bible was written in a real historical setting involving real people in a real culture. The passages that are enlightened by historical information are too numerous to detail, but we must constantly be aware that biblical events did not happen in a vacuum.

The second step in the exegetical process is *literary analysis*. We frequently hear people complain, "I was quoted out of context!" The biblical writers could surely make that complaint. Literary analysis is the attempt to place a verse of the Bible in its proper context by looking at the nature and flow of the larger piece of literature in which it is found. We can correctly understand passages of Scripture only as parts of their larger context. When you read a book for understanding, you don't just start in the middle on any page. Nor can we treat Scripture this way. Neither does one read one genre of literature just like every other. We understand poetry in one way, stories in another, and legislation in a different way still. Understanding the different kinds of literature in the Bible is crucial to asking the appropriate questions of the text.

Bible students have too frequently "ironed flat" the diverse literary landscape of the Word of God. Then they have proceeded to lay an artificial interpretive grid over sacred literature that permitted them to pick and choose rather indiscriminately. This method was then used to get words and sentences that they would then throw into a syllogism or other interpretive tool so they could generate a desired conclusion. We must show more integrity with the text God has placed in our hands.

For instance, most people are aware that the largest number of New Testament books are letters or epistles. As a distinctive literary type, letters are occasional documents. They speak to specific problems of specific people in specific places. We cannot read them as if they were sent directly to us. Otherwise, we may apply the instruction to a situation the author was not even addressing. We thereby harm both the original text and our present situation.

Consider the interpretation of poetry. We know that poetry often speaks in figurative language and thus cannot be read in the same way as an essay. Or what about the fascinating symbols of the book of Revelation? We strongly protest a kind of "proof-texting" that pulls verses out of the Bible without proper consideration of context and genre.

As with our earlier disclaimer concerning Christian apologetics, so do we now disavow any intent to offer this book as a treatise on exegetical process.[2] But it is imperative to understand that good theology can only result from sound exegesis, and we must be responsible and careful interpreters rather than "proof-texters" with the Bible. We take as axiomatic the contention of Fee and Stuart that the "only proper control for hermeneutics is to be found in the original intent of the biblical text"[3] and "a text cannot mean what it never meant."[4]

What we are essentially contending is that one should use the same basic skills in interpreting Scripture that would be used to understand any other piece of ancient or modern literature. Scripture cannot be read like the store catalog for the sake of finding what strikes one's fancy. This sort of subjectivism with the Word of God places the interpreter immediately *above* the sacred text to accept or reject according to taste rather than *beneath* its searching divine judgment and message of hope in Christ.

How to Apply Scripture

This brings us to the third and, for our purposes in this study, the most pressing question. How do we apply the biblical text to our contemporary situation? If there were an exact correspondence between our situation and a situation in Scripture,

---

2. For an excellent introduction to responsible handling of the various literary types of Scripture, see Gordon D. Fee and Douglas Stuart, *How to Read the Bible for All Its Worth* (Grand Rapids: Zondervan Publishing House, 1982).

3. Stuart and Fee, *How to Read the Bible*, p. 26.

4. Stuart and Fee, *How to Read the Bible*, p. 27.

there would be little problem. We could simply address it in the manner mandated by Scripture. But this is almost never the case. The distance between the culture of the Bible and our own modern culture is so great that there is seldom a clear correspondence.

Does this mean that Scripture has nothing to say today? Hardly, for as the Word of God it must still be relevant and binding. So what principle or principles allow us to move responsibly from the biblical world to our own?

We wish to argue that such principles are fundamentally theological. That is, they have to do with the nature of God and the relationship of humans and their world to him. Since God is unchanging in nature, principles derived from this source will always apply. The fullest and clearest revelation of God's person and nature is Jesus Christ. "In the past God spoke to our forefathers through the prophets at many times and in various ways, but in these last days he has spoken to us by his Son, whom he appointed heir of all things, and through whom he made the universe" (Heb. 1:1-2). Thus the person of Jesus as the revealer of the Father is the primary grid through which we read the New Testament documents. Our hermeneutic is therefore *theological* and *Christocentric*. Explicating what this means for the development of a modern ecclesiology is the goal of the remainder of this chapter.

Our beginning point is the general principle of Christ-centeredness, Christocentricity. The first question we must always ask in the process of the application of Scripture takes something of the following form: _Is the activity or methodology under contemplation consistent with the person and work of Jesus Christ? If we do this, will the people who see it think we reveal Christ? Will we be doing what people would expect to see Christ doing in this situation?_

This principle has broad consequences for ecclesiology. It says, for example, that the church need not have either explicit mandate or permission for everything it wishes to do. The church may confidently ground its activities of compassion and service in the character of her head. In his passionate appeal for simple acts of caring (cf. Matt. 25, _et al._), Jesus not only releases but compels the modern church to find incrementally more effective ways to feed the hungry, cloth the needy, minister to the outcasts, and provide homes for the homeless. Otherwise, we may discover that Jesus himself has become the castoff of our society. Literacy programs, soup kitchens, drug dependency programs, and prison outreaches need no other justification than that, in such activities, the church takes on both the heart and demeanor of the one she calls Lord and Master.

We are quick to admit that this principle will not answer all our hermeneutical questions (as the remainder of this chapter will make abundantly clear), but we are equally committed to the idea that this is where we must start. The task of Jesus was not salvation only; it was, as Hebrews 1:1-2 affirms, a revelation of God. His life was not an insignificant prelude to his all-important death. In his life he showed us how God thinks and acts. We learn from him what are matters of priority and what are matters of insignificance. Surely it is true that if every church paused to realign its programs, priorities, institutions, and convictions with the heart of Jesus, the kingdom would experience great gain.

This principle of Christocentricity is not as easy as it might appear. We must take care lest, instead of being conformed to the image of Christ, we impose our image on him. Then Jesus turns out to look just like us, placing his approval on what we have previously decided to do. This principle is not a blanket approval to confirm our prejudices. That is why the earlier exegetical step is so crucial. It gives the text its own integrity. We are not free to make Jesus into whatever we want or to make the text say what we wish it said.

A certain purity of heart is crucial here. Only an honest and open handling of the text can reveal to us who Jesus really is, especially at those points where a clear vision of Jesus calls into question our life or practice.

It is typically not too difficult to achieve agreement on some interpretive principle resembling the one specified above. But there are still many difficult questions we have not yet touched. Before proceeding further, we need to point out that all theological principles are binding, not just those specifically enfleshed by Jesus Christ. Insofar as Scripture reveals God, it must be heeded always and on all matters. We simply affirm, as all Christians do, the primacy of Jesus in this revelation process.

But if we affirm *theological principles* to be eternally binding and relevant, what about all the cultural forms and expressions contained in Scripture? God can only reveal himself to human beings in a human culture in a human language, but we believe these particular forms or expressions are binding if and only if they are inextricable from the theological principle of which they are an expression. Thus we reject a rigid "pattern theology" that simply proposes to transplant religious-cultural forms from the Bible to the 20th or 21st century. Such an attempt merely reproduces a particular human cultural expression and may lose the theological principle it was originally intended to convey.

Thus, if our general hermeneutic is Christocentricity, our specific hermeneutic for ecclesiology might be called *theological grounding*. A shorthand way of describing this interpretive mode would be as follows:

1. A bare historical precedent is not binding in and of itself.
2. Some historical precedents continue to be binding while others do not.
3. Theological truths are always binding but particular forms are binding only when their abandonment brings theological loss—and the retention of a form may actually result in theological obscurity in some cases.

This obviously requires some detailed explanation, so each of these points must be examined carefully.

"*A bare historical precedent is not binding in and of itself.*" This simply says that just because some Christian did something, sometime, somewhere, this is not of itself evidence that *every* Christian, in *every* time and *every* place also must do whatever it is we are talking about. If the form that this historical precedent instantiates is eternally binding, it is for some deeper reason than the mere fact that a Christian or group of Christians once did it. Something more significant than historical precedent must be produced to show that a practice witnessed in Scripture ought to be continued among us.

"*Some historical precedents continue to be binding while others do not.*" This simply recognizes that, in fact, some of what the early Christians did we feel compelled to continue to practice, while other precedents have long since been allowed to die. How do we make the decisions as to what must be preserved as crucial to the life of the church and what may be discarded without loss? It is the third statement that is intended to answer this question.

"*Theological truths are always binding but particular forms are binding only when their abandonment brings theological loss.*" Probably the simplest way to clarify this point is with some examples. Foot washing in the New Testament is a cultural expression of an eternally binding theological truth. Jesus shows us that it is of the very nature of God to be concerned for and to serve others. True greatness in the kingdom of God is found in humility and sacrificial service. This *does not* change. But how this self-giving service for other's sake is expressed *does* change. Foot washing simply does not have contemporary relevance as an expression of this theological truth. In fact, its occasional practice among some is seen as an eccentricity and thus defeats the purpose that was once embodied in the act. Foot washing as a form may be dispensed with, with no theological loss at all. Most religious traditions have acknowledged this by their practice, or in this case, lack of it. It can be replaced by a variety of other signs of service without loss to the theological truth it once embodied for people whose time and place were very different from ours.

Another example is the financial collectivism of the early Jerusalem church. From reading Acts 2, we find that they "had everything in common" (v. 44b). Most groups have made a *de facto* decision that this historical precedent is not binding, although some communal groups have deemed it so. What we want to emphasize is *how* such a decision ought to be made. Is there a theological principle here that must be preserved? We could argue for one. God, from the time of Israel onward, always insisted that the least well-off in the community of faith be cared for. Whether it was gleaning and tithing in the Old Testament or the communalism of Pentecost, this principle grows out of the very heart of God. But is the collectivism of this early church the only way to achieve such a goal? Of course not. While suitable to the unusual situation at Jerusalem, this approach was by no means universal in the early church. It therefore seems that the form (i.e., collectivism) is separable from the theological principle (i.e., care for the needy). If one disagreed with this, the only proper course of action would be to practice communalism.

We are convinced that some theological principles are so embedded or enmeshed with their forms that the form itself cannot be rejected without theological loss. We would contend that participation in the Lord's Supper is one such form. One cannot, in this case, do away with the form and preserve the principles it instantiates. They are inseparable. Jesus intended the ritual to be a kind of permanent connection of all Christians from the first century until the second coming in much the same way as Passover functions for the Jews. To abandon the ritual is to lose this connection. We will have more to say about the Lord's Supper and the principles it instantiates in a later chapter. For now, it must suffice to say that the Lord's Supper proclaims that all who are in Christ are a single community under the shadow of the cross. To abandon the practice of this communal meal would result in theological loss. It would, in fact, result in a loss of identity— just as the abandonment of Passover would result in a loss of identity for the Jews.

We do not deny that this recommended hermeneutical principle requires human judgement, but so do all other application principles. We feel the need to offer some explanation for why we preserve some practices and abandon others.

In the ecclesiology to be presented in this volume, there is a form of "patternism" present. It is not, however, the slavish imitation of everything the first-century Christian church said and did. It is instead a conscientious effort to honor in culturally appropriate ways the same eternal theological principles that they tried to embody—sometimes poorly, sometimes well—in their time.

It is likely clear to the reader that there are several levels at which disagreement with the approach we have offered can occur. We could have disagreement about the nature of Scripture. For those who see Scripture as a purely human document with no real divine authority, our passion to be biblical will seem unnecessary. Disagreement at this level is so basic that profitable discussion seems unlikely.

Disagreement is more likely to occur at the level of exegesis. Although these matters have an interest all their own, they are of little consequence to this study except where the divergent interpretations lead to differing theological principles.

Disagreement is most likely to occur at the level of application. Members of the various religious traditions—as well as those within a given tradition—will not always agree on how the theological principle at stake ought to be expressed in the modern world. What is called for here is understanding and discussion.

Most of us are convinced that we ought to be able to offer a theological defense for all our practices. If one wishes to contend for different practices, he or she is obligated to offer a sound theological justification. It is the responsibility of each religious tradition to raise questions continually about its thought and practice in light of Scripture so that the life of the church is anchored in eternal truths rather than the deep ruts of acculturated forms.

We started this chapter with the claim that Scripture is the anchor of the church. While we cannot hope to gain consensus for all the decisions we have made in our particular religious heritage, we hope to have drawn attention to what Scripture should do in the formation of an ecclesiology. It certainly does not present an absolute blueprint for building a church; it does, however, provide the theological parameters for such a project. In the final analysis, a defense of ecclesiastical practice must not be pragmatic but theological.

Conclusion

In summation, in our reading of Scripture we search for theological principles: eternal truths about God, man, and the world. Since these truths come in human culture and language, we use sound exegesis to decide what the author is really saying.

The practice of the church and personal Christian life are regulated by the theological principles we derive from sound exegesis. Since we always attempt to conform our belief and practice to the person of Jesus, we naturally place a priority on the Gospels and the Christological sections of the epistles. But we also take note of the early churches described in Acts and the epistles as they were attempting to become true communities of Christ.

We advocate attempting to conceive and model our churches on theological grounding. Sometimes this requires preservation of a particular form or practice; at other times, it does not. It is the preservation of the theological principles that allows us to claim continuity with the churches whose witness to Christ is recounted in the New Testament.

What we hope to gain from Scripture is primarily a vision of what a group of people committed to living under the Lordship of Jesus will be like. The apostolic witness in the early church is invaluable data for this quest. They knew Jesus Christ best and were committed, we believe, to a common project—to build churches not in their own image but in the image of Christ. We have no interest in building a first-century church or a 16th- or 19th- or even 20th-century church in the 21st century. To do so would elevate human culture to the status of divine truth. We hope, rather, to be led by Scripture to embody God's truth in ways that speak to our time and our place. Scripture demands no more, and we must be satisfied with no less.

Fundamental
Conceptions

CHAPTER THREE

Identity:
The Church as the
Body of Christ

There are many expressive metaphors in the
New Testament that reveal fascinating things
about the church. That it is God's house (i.e., family) indicates the acceptance and security that children feel in relation to a strong, protective father.
That it is Christ's bride connotes the loving intimacy that is shared voluntarily between partners.
That it is a vineyard points simultaneously to the
possibility for fruitfulness and the necessity of cul-
tivation. The itemization of these figures of speech
could go on and on.

No single metaphor used of the church can be
pressed to the exclusion of the others. Neither can
particular details of any metaphor nor some observation about the church under a biblical compari-
son be made the starting point for spinning out a
full theology of the church. With these qualifica-
tions and disclaimers in the record, we would ex-

plain our choice of one New Testament figure as
the organizing theme for this book about the
church.

Paul, the church's original theologian, used the
analogy of the church as *the body of Christ* to communicate fundamental insights about its nature.
Led of the Spirit in doing so, he employed this
metaphor again and again. It even appears that he
adapted it for the sake of particular points he was
seeking to make. Thus, disparities of a sort occur in
his application of it.

In writing to a church troubled by internal divisions, for example, he used the concept to appeal
for harmonious functioning of its various members. In the process of developing his theme of one
body composed of many members, he allowed the
body's "head" to represent a rival member who
feels no need for certain other members who are
represented as the body's "feet" (1 Cor. 12:21b). In
the epistle we call Ephesians, however, the same
apostle employed the figure of the church as a
body and affirmed that Christ himself is its "head"
(Eph. 1:22).

There is no doctrinal disparity in this versatile
use of the church-as-body figure. It is simply a reflection of the flexibility of a metaphor.

Impressed as we are with Paul's unique use of
this analogy, we have chosen to build from it in trying to offer a contemporary theology of the church.
While some biblical figures of speech do not communicate very well to our culture (e.g., vineyards,
lamps hidden under bowls, etc.), this one is both
timeless and trans-cultural. We will dare to employ

it freely, then, but we will do so while making a conscious attempt to do theology from the careful application of the hermeneutical principles discussed in Chapter Two and employing the church-as-body metaphor only as a communications device. Theology must build on the bedrock of biblical principle and not on the manipulation of a literary device.

The *task* of this chapter is to explore the identity of the church revealed in the New Testament. Its *thesis* is that the church's identity is inseparable from Jesus Christ himself and that the church must discover and affirm its identity in him. The *goal* of this chapter is to focus believers on the person and work of Christ as the starting point for discovering what the church is supposed to be.

The Greatest Compliment

In a pastoral statement of concern for his spiritual charges, Paul reported his continual prayerfulness on their behalf. In the context of that report, he offered beautiful lines of adoration for the Lord Jesus Christ and paid the church its greatest compliment in Scripture.

> I pray also that the eyes of your heart may be enlightened in order that you may know the hope to which he has called you, the riches of his glorious inheritance in the saints, and his incomparably great power for us who believe. That power is like the working of his mighty strength, which he exerted in Christ when he raised him from the dead and seated him at

his right hand in the heavenly realms, far above all rule and authority, power and dominion, and every title that can be given, not only in the present age but also in the one to come. And God placed all things under his feet and appointed him to be head over everything for *the church, which is his body, the fullness of him* who fills everything in every way (Eph. 1:18-23).

The astonishing tribute to the church in this text comes to a focus around its role as the body of Christ which is the "fullness" (*pleroma* = fulfillment, rounding out, completion) to Jesus who is the "[one] who fills" (*pleroumenou* = makes full, rounds out, completes) all things in every way.

Dare we believe it? Is it too bold for us to affirm? Does the church have such a relationship to Jesus that it provides something that is necessary to him? It is easy and natural to affirm that Christ supplies our needs. Is it blasphemy to hold that the church supplies his?

In order to understand Paul and lest his statement be misunderstood to claim too much for the church, we must examine three critical terms.

The Church as *Ekklesia*

Our English word "church" translates the Greek term *ekklesia*.[1] In the New Testament, it occurs 114 times. Over half of these instances are in the writ-

---

1. Cf. *Theological Dictionary of the New Testament*, 1965 ed., s.v. "*ekklesia*," by K. L. Schmidt, pp. 501-36; *New International Dictionary of New Testament Theology*, 1975 ed., s.v., "Church, Synagogue," by L. Coenen, pp. 291-307.

ings of Paul. The meaning of the word is, as in pre-Christian literature, "assembly" or "meeting." It is not used in our modern sense of society, denomination, organization, or religious club. Our English term "church" clearly carries implications for the modern mind that never belonged to *ekklesia*. Can anyone imagine Paul asking a Christian brother he just met, "And of what church are you a member?" The New Testament *ekklesia* is the assembly of people God has called out of the world by the gospel to be constituted his kingdom citizens.

When Paul writes to the "church of the Thessalonians" (1 Thess. 1:1), it seems clear that he envisions the Christians of that city called into assembly. Thus he can ask that his letter be "read to all the brothers" (1 Thess. 5:27). In his correspondence to Corinth, the idea of the church is clearly that of a particular group in association. The specific idea of an assembly is certainly in view at 1 Corinthians 11:18 ("when you come together as a church") and 14:35 ("it is disgraceful for a woman to speak in the church"). Even when he used the plural of the word, the idea was still that of local assemblies of Christians (cf. 1 Cor. 16:1; Gal. 1:22; 1 Thess. 2:14; 2 Thess. 1:4; *et al.*).

There are also instances, however, where Paul speaks of something larger than a house church or local assembly. Primary among these texts would be the paragraph quoted above from Ephesians 1. When the affirmation about Christ is that God has "appointed him to be head over everything for the church" (v. 22), the church is to be understood as the collective assembly of people who are full citi-

zens of the kingdom of heaven (cf. Eph. 2:6; Col.
3:1; Phil. 3:20a). These people have been called out
of darkness into light, out of Satan's rule into the
rule of God.

One does not cease to be part of the church
when the body of believers with whom he has
shared a spiritual experience disperses at the end
of an assembly. She is still a functioning part of the
church which is that body of people called unto God
and charged with representing him in this world.

In what sense, however, does the *ekklesia* "represent" God in the world? That leads to a second
term that is important to a correct understanding
of the church's identity.

The Church as *Soma Christou*

When Paul writes of the church as Christ's
"body," English versions are translating the word
soma.[2] Its use in the New Testament reflects a
wide range of meaning. *Soma* may be a corpse
(Matt. 27:52) or a living body (Mark 5:29). In texts
such as James 2:16, the physical nature of a
human body stands at the forefront. Yet the body is
clearly more than a physical organism and signifies
instead the totality of one's person.

In atonement passages such as Hebrews 10:10
and 1 Peter 2:24, the referent for *soma* is not
merely Jesus' physical body but his entire person.
Thus to say that believers "have been made holy

---

2. Cf. *Theological Dictionary of the New Testament*, 1971 ed., s.v.
"soma, somatikos, sussomos" by Schweizer, pp. 1024-94; *New
International Dictionary of New Testament Theology*, 1975 ed., s.v.,
"Body (*Soma*)" by J. A. Motyer, pp. 232-42.

through the sacrifice of the body of Jesus Christ" or that the Son of God "bore our sins in his body on the tree" is to affirm the act of his total self-giving for our sakes.

In the writings of Paul, *soma* refers to the complete person, a being in totality, man as a whole. The reference is not to a mere shell or external impediment; it is to the very essence of one's personhood. For Paul, human beings have identity as bodies. "Man does not *have* a *soma*; he *is soma*."[3] In our physical instantiation and particularity, we exist.

Paul's general rule was to use the term *soma* for incarnate personality in its entirety. Thus he could affirm that our very bodies are "members of Christ himself" (1 Cor. 6:15) and that each disciple's body is "a temple of the Holy Spirit" (1 Cor. 6:19). He admitted that he had to discipline his own body (1 Cor. 9:27) and appealed to his fellow Christians to "offer [their] bodies as living sacrifices" to God (Rom. 12:1).

Body, then, was not extraneous to personhood for Paul. And this point becomes critical when one moves to the Pauline use of *soma* to characterize the church in relation to Christ. For him, the church was not something to be conceived as extrinsic to Christ or irrelevant to him. Neither was the church merely the sum of its parts. A fundamental statement of his view of the church as Christ's *soma* is found in the Corinthian correspondence: "The body is a unit, though it is made up of many parts; and though all its parts are many,

---

3. R. Bultmann, *Theology of the New Testament, I*, trans. by Kendrick Grobel (New York: Charles Scribner's Sons, 1951), p. 194.

they form one body. So it is with Christ. For we were all baptized by one Spirit into one body—whether Jews or Greeks, slave or free—and we were all given the one Spirit to drink" (1 Cor. 12:12-13).

The notion of the body as a unit is not limited here to the various corporeal parts (i.e., believers) who are set in place by God to be hands, feet, eyes, etc. Its oneness consists as well in the fact that the One Spirit animates the One Body as his proper sphere of operation. In his church, we are an in-Spirited body or, if one prefers, an incarnation of the divine Spirit. Just as the invisible God made himself visible and tangible in Jesus Christ, so the now-invisible Christ is making himself visible and tangible to the world through his church.

As the rite of initiation into Christ's spiritual body, baptism is meaningless as mere water. The effective agent of baptism as a spiritual ordinance is not water but the attending Holy Spirit. Jesus spoke to Nicodemus of the new birth as a single action with two elements. "Unless a man is born of water and the Spirit," he told the Jewish ruler, "he cannot enter the kingdom of God" (John 3:5). All persons, whether Jews or Gentiles, who have become one body by the experience of the one baptism and who have received the gift of the one Spirit, collectively constitute a unit under the direction of the head, Jesus Christ. If there is legitimacy to Paul's metaphor and the theological rationale behind it, there is at least some sense in which we may call Christ's church a *second incarnation*.

God was incarnate once through the birth of a babe at Bethlehem and lived out the personal meaning of "God with us" in a hostile environment. He has condescended to be incarnate once again through a fellowship larger than any geographical boundaries or sectarian divisions in order to achieve the societal meaning of "God with us" in a still-hostile environment.

In the first incarnation, a bodily presence was a practical necessity for his mission. "Since the children have flesh and blood, he too shared in their humanity so that by his death he might destroy him who holds the power of death—that is, the devil—and free those who all their lives were held in slavery by their fear of death" (Heb. 2:14-15).

In the second incarnation, a bodily presence remains a practical necessity for his mission. Since he is still working on behalf of human beings rather than angels (cf. Heb. 2:16), he still needs a point of contact with the world that is tangible and concrete. Thus we are not asked to believe in and mystically participate in an ethereal abstraction called the church, but we are invited to be part of an objective experience that involves us as directly with him as a body is concerned with its head. Just as he functioned in the world via his physical body in the first incarnation, we see him functioning in the world today through his spiritual body in the second incarnation.

It is only against this background that the third critical term from our original text can be accepted of the church.

The Church as *Pleroma*

The outrageous nature of Paul's claim about the church strikes us still. He wrote that the church is "the fullness of him who fills everything in every way." That Jesus Christ fills up and brings to completion all the divine purposes is an anticipated affirmation from so Christ-intoxicated a writer as Paul. But how dare he make Christ's fullness depend in any way upon this divine-human enterprise known as the church!

The church is flawed. It is weakened by division. Its call to holiness is belied by what we know of the manifest impurities of some and the secret sins of all. Yet, in some sense that needs to be clarified for us, it is Christ's fullness in the world.

"Fullness" is the English translation of *pleroma*.[4] The Greek term has a wide range of meaning in the New Testament. It can refer to "that which fills" and therefore indicates a patch on an old garment (Mark 2:21) or food scraps that filled up several baskets (Mark 6:43; 8:20). Used in an active sense, it can signify the act of bringing a thing to fullness (i.e., "fulfillment," Rom. 13:10); used in a passive sense, it can point to that which has been brought to fullness (i.e., "fulfillment," 1 Cor. 10:11).

It is the possibility of understanding *pleroma* in either an active or passive sense that causes commentators to part company on its meaning in

4. Cf. *Theological Dictionary of the New Testament*, 1968 ed., s.v. *"pleroma"* by Delling, pp. 298-305; *New International Dictionary of New Testament Theology*, 1975 ed., s.v. "Fullness (*pleroo*)" by R. Schippers, pp. 733-741.

Ephesians 1:23. Are we to understand Paul to say
that the church somehow brings about a fullness to
Christ? Or are we to understand him as stating the
less controversial and obviously true fact that the
church is brought to fullness by Christ?

In Colossians 1:19 and 2:9, the word *pleroma* is
used of Christ in relation to the entire Godhead.
The unambiguous statement of these texts is that
the fullness of deity is embodied in Jesus Christ.
"For God was pleased to have all his fullness dwell
in him." "For in Christ all the fullness of the Deity
lives in bodily form."

It is immediately apparent that the church cannot have the relationship to Christ that Christ has
to the Godhead. Christ is a perfect receptacle for
divine fullness because he is deity in his own person. He can both bear and represent faithfully all
the divine graces because they are natural to him.
The same cannot be said of the church, though, for
whatever holiness the church may exhibit to the
world is the result of a process that can hardly be
described as natural to the men and women who
collectively compose it.

At this point, however, students of Scripture
must be warned again about pressing a metaphor
too hard. Indeed, it overtaxes (perhaps abandons)
the figure of the church as Christ's body to read it
as a parallel relationship to that between the
Godhead and Christ. The fear that Christ will be
portrayed as somehow deficient in his person if the
church is allowed to stand as his "fullness" forgets
the essential complementarity of the head-body figure. A head is incomplete without a body, and a

body is incomplete without a head. To step outside this single metaphor and to spin a theology of the church as indispensable to the personal completeness of the eternal Christ would be unjustified. At the same time, to fail to grasp the point intended by this metaphor would also be unjustified.

While Christ *in his person* is altogether complete without the church, Christ *in his earthly function* is incomplete without his spiritual body, the church.

In his incarnation at Bethlehem, he accepted limitations to which he had never been subject in his heavenly status. He was omnipresent in eternity, but he was not present in Jerusalem while in his family home at Nazareth. In his humanity, he voluntarily limited himself in certain ways without forfeiting his deity.

In his second incarnation through the church, he has done the same thing. He has accepted limitations that are not obligatory. Though perfect in his holiness, he has voluntarily chosen to function to certain ends through his church on Earth. He could communicate the gospel message to unbelievers by a celestial voice, through angelic mediation, or by telepathic disclosure. Without any forfeiture of fullness in his person, however, he has chosen to convey the lifestyle and message of salvation through human agency. In that sense, the church is indeed the *pleroma* of Christ. We are called to complete, execute, and perform in our collective life what he desires to have done in the world. What he *would* do in our world, we *must* do in order to be faithful as his body.

Remaining within the figure of speech Paul selected, the head functions through the various parts of the whole body of which it is the preeminent member. If the head wishes to change its location slightly, it activates the neck and chest muscles; if it wishes to change locations more radically, it initiates a complex series of activities that will result in the feet moving the entire body. If the head wishes to communicate, it employs the mouth. If it chooses to take something to itself, it mobilizes the hands as an extension of that choice.

It is the same with the church as Christ's body. The church is the body that implements the will of the head. Thus the *ekklesia* functions as Christ's *soma* and provides his *pleroma* in the world.

Though we may think ourselves too sophisticated as adults to rehearse the lesson many of us were taught in Sunday School, it is nevertheless true that Jesus Christ wills to employ our feet to take him where the world is hurting, to use our hands to bind up the wounds left by sin, and to speak through our lips to declare the fullness of the Father's love.

Understood in this active sense, we complete our interpretation of Ephesians 1:23 and discover the greatest compliment ever paid the church. Christ is the church's Savior and the one who brings all things to their completion and fullness. Yet, by virtue of his sovereign and gracious choice, he has decided to function in the world through his body, the church. Just as he was God incarnate in a physical body as Jesus of Nazareth, so is he now God incarnate in a spiritual body as the church.

When that church is healthy and engaged in its
proper work, it becomes Christ's very presence in
the world. It carries on what he started among us.
It is the grand finale to his ministry and is his chosen vehicle for living in the world in fullness rather
than in mere memory.

In the late William Barclay's popular-level introduction to the book of Acts, there is a memo-
rable section that makes this point with consider-
able poignancy. He wrote:

> In one sense it is the whole lesson of the
> Book of Acts that the life of Jesus goes on *in*
> *His Church.* Dr. John Foster tells how an in-
> quirer from Hinduism came to an Indian
> Bishop. All unaided he had read the New
> Testament, and the story had fascinated him
> and Christ had laid His spell upon him. "Then
> he read on . . . and felt he had entered into a
> new world. In the gospels it was Jesus, His
> works and His suffering. In the Acts . . . what
> the disciples did and thought and taught had
> taken the place that Christ had occupied. The
> Church continued where Jesus had left off at
> His death. 'Therefore,' said this man to me, 'I
> must belong to *the Church that carries on the*
> *life of Christ.*'" The Book of Acts tells of the
> Church that carries on the life of Christ.[5]

That's it! We are called to belong to the church
that carries on the life of Christ. To be his Spirit-

5. William Barclay, *The Acts of the Apostles* (Philadelphia:
Westminster Press, 1955), p. 2.

filled presence in the world. To do what he would be doing if he were still among us in a physical body.

Personal Focus for the Church

If this understanding of the nature of the church were predominant among believers, it would reorient our thinking in a revolutionary way. It would focus our attention on Jesus himself as the model for the church to imitate in the world.

In his lived experience and work among us, Jesus Christ is the standard for the church. Abandoning the tendency to "compare ourselves with ourselves," we must judge ourselves individually and our function as the church solely in relationship to the Lord Jesus. We are truly the church only when we are living with him as the head and drawing our life force from his indwelling Spirit.

The point of reference for understanding "all that Jesus began to do and to teach until the day he was taken up to heaven" (Acts 1:1b-2a) is the apostolic witness preserved in Scripture. In the words just quoted, Luke—the only Gentile writer of New Testament materials and the only Gospel writer to produce a sequel to his faith-tract on Jesus—was pointing Theophilus back to the gospel data. In his second volume, Luke proposed to write a summary history of the spread of Christianity from Jerusalem into the larger Roman world (Acts 1:8). What Luke provided us are occasional glimpses of the church's attempt to carry on what Jesus started. Some of the episodes are glorious and exciting, worthy of the Christ in whose name they were done. Many others, however, are depressing and second-rate, altogether unworthy of Christ.

Because the church must discover and affirm its identity in Christ, we must begin at the beginning. We must focus on who Jesus was and what he did in order to be his body rather than on the history of churches that have given us only occasional and always imperfect peeks at his glory. The body must look to its head for identity rather than grope for some sense of self-awareness either in the first, twelfth, or eighteenth century.

While we dare not ignore anything the New Testament documents tell us about the doctrine, worship, and life of the church, we must learn first of the person whose life that church was attempting to perpetuate. While the study of subsequent church history will provide us with insights that alternately reassure and warn us, we must be careful of history's limitations. If it is possible to see Christ himself, we will be better advised to attempt our own modeling of his presence in the world from that vision rather than through defective representations that antedate our own.

The point of all this is to try to pry our thinking away from an *institutional focus* to a *personal focus*. The church is not merely an institution; if it were, it could be called into being as the sum total of its doctrinal-behavioral components as witnessed in Acts and the epistles. The church is also an organism; its identity must be discovered experientially where a body of men and women live together in "the grace of the Lord Jesus Christ, and the love of God, and the fellowship of the Holy Spirit" (2 Cor. 13:14).

For the sake of clarity, we mean for the term "institutional focus" to carry the common notion of defining the church by means of its external marks. The church has doctrine, worship, ordinances, etc. But is that enough? Most of us have encountered—or been part of—a group that had all the "marks" of being a church but left us feeling cold and distant from Christ (cf. Rev. 2:4). By contrast, we mean for the term "personal focus" to signify the presence of Christ as Lord within the body. Of course there will be certain "marks of the church" present in that fellowship for all to observe. But there will also be much more. There will be the compassion, vibrancy, and healing power of Christ at work among all who are part of its life.

Another revolutionary thing that would result from an understanding of the church as Christ's body would be a shifting of allegiances. Denominational loyalty could give way to loyalty to Christ. Sectarian divisions within a given fellowship could be overcome as line-item theology gives way to Christ-centered interpretation of Scripture. Commitment to a local church could become a means to the end of commitment to Christ and not an alternative to it. For the purpose of formulating a theology of the church that has any hope of surviving in the century ahead, this sort of switch in loyalty must take place.

If our understanding of the church remains institutional in focus, division and party rivalry remain inevitable. If we manage to realign our thinking in order to make it more consistent with the

New Testament ideal of body-to-head association, the possibility of loving forbearance among the members of the body can become a reality.

When Christ becomes all in all to us, our imperfect approximations of him in our personal lives and in our corporate experiences will be seen for what they are—imperfect approximations. We will be released from the tendency to judge one another and will be free to encourage one another to growth in Christ.

"And he is the head of the body, the church; he is the beginning and the firstborn from among the dead, so that in everything he might have the supremacy" (Col. 1:18). That the supremacy has not been reserved for Christ through the history of the church hardly needs to be proved. Unconditional submission to some earthly leader has produced sins ranging from idolatrous worship of mortals to mass hysteria to group suicide. Claims by a group to be the sole repository of or channel for God's truth on Earth have generated sins ranging from the Inquisition to denominational rivalry to personal arrogance.

Christians and faithful churches have the responsibility to judge between truth and error. Both have the duty to warn against false teaching that dismantles the gospel (cf. 2 John 7-11) or leads to sinful behavior (cf. 1 Tim. 6:3-10). More often than not, however, the history of the church traces rivalries over eschatological theories and church property rather than over fundamentals of the Christian faith.

As opposed to this tendency to conflict and division, believers have been called to harmony. "Let the peace of Christ rule in your hearts, since as members of one body you were called to peace" (Col. 3:15). Again, however, the secret to harmony is found in the understanding of the church as Christ's "one body" rather than as an institution whose vested interests must be protected by human power plays.

In a passage mentioned early in this chapter, Paul expanded the theme of the unity of the people of God under this very figure of the church as a body.

> The body is a unit, though it is made up of many parts; and though all its parts are many, they form one body. So it is with Christ. For we were all baptized by one Spirit into one body—whether Jews or Greeks, slave or free—and we were all given the one Spirit to drink.
>
> Now the body is not made up of one part but of many. . . . But in fact God has arranged the parts in the body, every one of them, just as he wanted them to be. If they were all one part, where would the body be? As it is, there are many parts, but one body.
>
> The eye cannot say to the hand, "I don't need you!" And the head cannot say to the feet, "I don't need you!" . . . If one part suffers, every part suffers with it; if one part is honored, every part rejoices with it.
>
> Now you are the body of Christ, and each one of you is a part of it (1 Cor. 12:12-27; cf. Rom. 12:4-8).

The obvious diversity we encounter in the body of Christ frightens us until we realize that unity and uniformity are not equivalent terms. The notion of many parts with varieties of function is fully consistent with the understanding of the church as Christ's body. That diversity is frightening only when we are thinking in terms of a monolithic institution. In a living organism, there can be unity in diversity. In an inflexible institution, diversity can only be disruptive.

Thus we plead for an understanding of the church's identity as the spiritual body of Christ. Many things about the nature, mission, and function of the church that will be said in later chapters of this book will make sense only against this background understanding of its identity. With many others before us, we plead for keener awareness that the church

> exists in order to pour out its life in service— healing the sick, casting out demons, cleansing lepers, restoring sight for the blind, providing food for the hungry, giving rest to the weary, making homes for the homeless, bringing comfort to the distraught, preaching peace to those near and far. Like Jesus himself, it lives by dying, pouring out its life to satisfy human need wherever and in whatever form it finds it.[6]

Setting aside the obvious confusion some create by equating the church with a building, the still

6. E. Glenn Hinson, *The Church: Design for Survival* (Nashville: Broadman Press, 1967), p. 35.

commoner mistake is to equate the church with whatever it is that we are at the moment. It is often counter-productive when unbelievers see us and equate Christ with some of the things we are doing. And it is both deceptive and discouraging when we see ourselves and our activities as a definition of the church.

By the mistake of defining the church in terms of function, we come up with today's stereotypes of institutional activities. Thus the church is a group of people in assembly to praise the Lord. It is devoted Christians preaching the gospel. It is compassionate people feeding hungry children or tending the sick. Or the church may be narrow-minded bigots. Or cold-hearted, insensitive people. Or simply people who are fundamentally no different in life concerns from everyone else around them.

These flattering or unflattering images of church folk and their behavior define the church for many people. But these descriptions of church behaviors no more identify the church than Michaelangelo's sculpture defines David or Carl Sandburg's writing defines Abraham Lincoln. Whatever success Michaelangelo achieved in sculpting David or Sandburg in producing a biography of Lincoln, awareness of their work is not the same as knowing their subjects.

Something of the same thing is at work with reference to the identity of the church. When we have studied the life of the early church, we have examined first-century attempts to depict Christ to the world. What we find there must always be compared to Christ in his person as we can know him through the total apostolic witness. When we have sorted out correct doctrine for ourselves about entering the church, worshipping as the church, governing the church, and a dozen other subjects, we may think we have established the church's identity. It would be possible to do all this with care and precision and never identify the church. Worse still, it would be possible to spell out our beliefs on all these issues and never experience Christ.

There is neither a set of doctrines nor a series of activities that can guarantee the existence of the church. No sequence of rituals or election of a governing body distinguishes it with certainty. All these features are to the identity of the church what marble and printer's ink are to the identities of David and Abraham Lincoln. They are marks, shadows, and expressive representations of certain features of the church. But the church is something distinct still.

What religious people of all stripes and varieties have done in an effort to determine the identity of the church seems to make perfectly good sense. We have studied the New Testament book of Acts in great detail, along with critical sections of certain New Testament epistles such as Ephesians and Colossians. We have extracted doctrines, organizational patterns, and the like. The results of our research have been regarded as norms or standards. Then we have attempted to translate those norms into our own experience. To do so, we have assumed, would be to create (or restore) the church of the New Testament.

But there is no perfect church to study as a model for imitation. Jerusalem was racially narrow and biased. Colosse was tainted with doctrinal heresy. Corinth was beset with immoral behavior. What we must realize is that *there is no finality for the church in any of its corporate manifestations*. When most of us speak of *the church*, we speak either of some unrealized ideal that is a mere abstraction or of a deficient institution with which we have had personal (and possibly frustrating) experience.

Even if there were a perfect church, our proper task would not be to reproduce its forms but to capture for ourselves its vision of modeling Christ and to be as faithful to that vision as that perfect church had been. We would thus follow Christ as that church had followed him. Our relationship with the Savior would be a direct one rather than one mediated through that church. To set as our goal the reproduction of a given first-, tenth-, or eighteenth-century church as the means to being Christ's body would be as unwise upon reflection as someone's misguided belief that buying a house, furniture, and car like those of his happily married friend will provide him a good marriage. That man should put his energies into finding a woman to love rather than into building and decorating. Similarly, our goal of being the body of Christ must derive from a personal relationship with him rather than from a reproduction of form, ritual, and methodology.

Some Practical Implications

The remainder of this book will be our attempt to work through some of the practical implications of this view of the church as "his body, the fullness of him who fills everything in every way." For the present, only a cursory overview of some additional postulates to our thesis must suffice.

First, the head must govern the body, not vice versa. In this day of consumer-oriented religion, this point can be lost quickly. Christ is God; we are mortals. Christ is King; we are his subjects. Christ is Savior; we are sinners. Christ is Head; we are his body.

Second, the goal of the body is the glorification of the head. Saved and made alive by grace, God's redeemed people are "created in Christ Jesus to do good works" that reflect glory to Christ and not to ourselves (cf. Eph. 2:1-10; Matt. 5:16).

Third, the various members of the body are loved by the head. When Paul was persecuting the church, Jesus confronted him on the Damascus Road and said, "Saul! Saul! Why do you persecute me? . . . I am Jesus of Nazareth, whom you are per-secuting" (Acts 22:7b-8; cf. Matt. 25:40,45). How was Saul mistreating Jesus? By threatening and harming his body. The head loves all the members of the body.

Fourth, the diverse members of the body love one another. Indeed, "each member belongs to all the others" (Rom. 12:5b). "If one part suffers, every part suffers with it; if one part is honored, every part rejoices with it" (1 Cor. 12:26). We are a broth-erhood, a fellowship, a *koinonia*. The fact that we love one another is a down-to-earth proof of our heavenly regeneration (cf. 1 John 4:7-8).

Fifth, the body is destined to share the fate of its head. "And if the Spirit of him who raised Jesus from the dead is living in you, he who raised Christ from the dead will also give life to your mortal bodies through his Spirit, who lives in you" (Rom. 8:11). After our present participation in his ministry, sufferings, and joy, there still remains an everlasting participation in his glory.

Conclusion

If the thesis of this chapter has not struck you yet as a drastic and pregnant one, the forthcoming chapters will make its meaning clearer. We have proposed a shift from institution to person, pattern to principle, deed to motivation. It is an affirmation of grace over our tendency to find and bind rules. It is an affirmation of freedom, under Christ's headship, over bondage to an imagined prototype or blueprint for the church.

Why are we the church? Is it just because we have duplicated a pattern? No, but because we have been made alive in Christ. To be the church is the meaning of our new life, to live as his spiritual body in the world.

Why should the church participate in a ceremony called the Lord's Supper? Do we do it because we are obliged to follow the example of the churches at Troas and Corinth? No, but because it is a means of entering more deeply into the experience of Jesus Christ, of participating in his body and blood.

Why ought the church to be concerned about the homeless or people in jails? Is it simply because we are commanded to do it? No, but because serving them is a means of ministering to Jesus himself.

Why should the church evangelize? Do we share our faith only because we fear to stand before the Lord and answer for the failure to do so? No, but because we possess the eternal riches of the kingdom of God within our fellowship and are compelled by love to share them with others.

The commands remain in Scripture. The examples of the earliest saints are recorded for our instruction. There are surely some patterns and steps and structures to be discerned in Scripture. But none of these—nor all of them taken together—constitutes the church. They do not form the essence of the church. They do not make life within the church meaningful, desirable, or attractive to outsiders.

To pass from the infancy stage of learning our duties and performing them from fear to the level of being "mature, attaining to the whole measure of the fullness of Christ" (Eph. 4:13b) is to pass from darkness into light. It is to make the transition from death into life. It is to move away from a religious club that can perpetuate itself by gimmicks into the church that lives because of its vital link to the Son of God.

The church as it was intended to be exists only when Christ has the supremacy in everything for us and is at the head of a redeemed body of people who are filled with his Spirit. We dare to claim finality only for Christ himself and for no corporate or individual attempt to declare him. The ancient claim "The Christian religion is Jesus Christ" is not wide of the mark. The rallying cry "No creed but Christ" is fundamentally sound. To articulate the broad outline of this approach is the goal of this volume. To instantiate it in our world is the ongoing challenge to Christ's disciples until he comes.

CHAPTER FOUR

Nature:
A Pilgrim Church and the
Kingdom of God

One is struck rather quickly by the chasm that exists between the exalted talk of the last chapter and one's lived experience in the church. We may indeed acknowledge Christ as our head and mentor, but we are often poor examples of our lofty theology.

This is not just true of our present age but seems always to have been the case. To recognize this fact honestly and forthrightly helps us avoid some remarkably sinister pitfalls. Perhaps the most scathing rebuke that any of the seven churches of Asia received was reserved for the church of Laodicea. What was its problem? The risen Christ analyzed its situation: "You say 'I am rich. I have acquired wealth and do not need a thing.' But you do not realize that you are wretched, pitiful, poor, blind, and naked" (Rev. 3:17). The most sinister sin of all may be for the church to fail to realize her insufficiency and neediness.

The all-sufficiency of the Christian is found in
Jesus Christ. In its historical reality, the church of
Jesus Christ is woefully insufficient. Though it is
the spiritual body of Christ, it is composed of sinful-though-saved human beings. The church is
surely insufficient as a reflection of Jesus' holiness,
love, and glory to the world. It is insufficient to accomplish the things that need to be done in the
world. And it is altogether insufficient in its own
power to save anyone.

Whatever degree of sufficiency the church has is
related to a limited and narrow function. It is sufficient to be what God has called it to be in this
fallen world. It is sufficient to serve as a haven of
fellowship for struggling believers who bear with
and support one another to grow in the grace and
knowledge of the Lord. It is sufficient to lift up
Christ so his all-sufficiency can draw people to
himself for salvation.

The church is not a hospital, school, motel, publishing house, restaurant, or addiction-treatment
center. Yet particular local churches may need to
employ or create one or more of these entities so as
to lift up Jesus and address the needs it sees.
Other churches may never need or choose to draw
on any of them. Under the all-sufficient Christ,
each congregation decides what is necessary to
achieve its goals. As different congregations attempt to honor Christ and to meet the needs they
encounter, their members will discover their insufficiency repeatedly and learn to appreciate the all-
sufficiency of their Lord.

If salvation were our own accomplishment, perhaps we would feel compelled to affirm the church's

all-sufficiency. Because it is by grace through faith, we are not forced into such an absurd and arrogant posture. We are free to confess our inadequacy and to affirm all-sufficiency for Christ alone.

A Pilgrim Church

The thesis of this chapter is quite simply that the nature of the church is that of a pilgrim. The pilgrim church is never a static accomplishment, but always a moving process. In this life the church never arrives but is forever on the journey. The church is never a perfect reflection of God's ideal but always strives to move toward that goal expressed in Scripture by the words "kingdom of God." The relationship between the pilgrim church and the kingdom of God is articulated well by Hans Kung:

> Even though it is not the kingdom of God which is to come, it is already under the reign of God which has begun; though looking forward to the final victory of the reign of God, it can look back to the decisive victory: in Jesus the Christ. . . . The meaning of the Church does not reside in itself, in what it is, but in what it is moving towards. It is the reign of God which the Church hopes for, bears witness to, proclaims. It is not the bringer or the bearer of the reign of God which is to come and is at the same time already present, but its voice, its announcer, its herald. God alone can bring his reign; the Church is devoted entirely to [the kingdom's] service.[1]

---

1. Hans Kung, *The Church*, (Garden City, NY: Image Books, 1976), pp. 134-135.

We cannot trace the concept of the reign of God through Scripture here, but we do need to draw attention to several points made in the paragraph just cited. First, Scripture pictures the kingdom as both a present reality to be experienced and a future event to be anticipated. A pair of passages from Luke may help show the dual nature of the kingdom. In Luke 11:2, in his Model Prayer, Jesus prays for the coming of the kingdom. But in Luke 17:20-21, in a discussion with the Pharisees, we find this curious conversation: "Once, having been asked by the Pharisees when the kingdom of God would come, Jesus replied, 'The kingdom of God does not come visibly, nor will people say, "Here it is" or "There it is," because the kingdom of God is within you [or, among you].'" Here Jesus seems to indicate that the kingdom was already in their midst.

If someone thinks the Luke 17 text is merely a reference to the kingdom's essence without reference to time, there is no doubt about the present reality of the kingdom being affirmed in Matthew 12:28. In a controversy with the Pharisees over his activity in casting out demons, Jesus said: "But if I drive out demons by the Spirit of God, then the kingdom of God has come upon you." In his own person and work, the kingdom of heaven had broken into human experience.

But the future aspect of the kingdom is indicated in such texts as Mark 9:1, Luke 22:18, and 1 Thessalonians 3:13 and 4:15. How should we understand this dual nature?

Perhaps a couple of diagrams will help clarify the picture. If the following represented the situation, the kingdom would be entirely future.

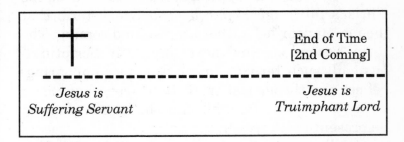

But of course this does not fully represent the biblical picture. Now, consider the following more complete diagram.

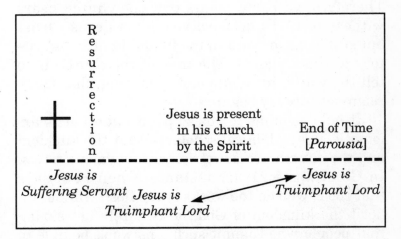

Now it becomes clearer why the kingdom is both present and future. The reign of Christ was inaugurated in connection with his personal victory over sin and Satan, as verified at his resurrection, and he reigns now in his church; but the consummation of this reign occurs at the end of time when every knee will bow and every tongue confess that Jesus is Lord. The typical word used to describe Christ's full reign is *parousia*, a Greek term that means "appearing" rather than second coming. The term "second coming" never occurs in Scripture.[2] Instead, such terms as *parousia* (i.e., appearing) reflect the theological truth that Jesus has never really gone away from his church. He continues to be present in it through the Spirit.

So Christians live between the times. We look back to the triumph of God over the powers of darkness at the resurrection, and we look forward to the end of time when God will be all in all. Therefore, as Kung points out, the church bears witness to God's decisive victory in Jesus Christ but still looks forward to the final and ultimate victory of the kingdom. The task of the church is to tell the world, in its life and preaching, that God's reign has already begun.

It only remains for us to point out what is axiomatic among biblical scholars—that the kingdom and the church are not strictly synonymous terms. In Galatians 5:21, for instance, when Paul says that those who do the works of the flesh will not inherit the kingdom of God, he is surely not saying that people who commit such sins won't be able to get in the church.

---

2. The closest thing to the term "second coming" in the New Testament is found at Hebrews 9:28b. "[Christ] will appear a second time, not to bear sin, but to bring salvation to those who are waiting for him."

Although the relationship is not one of identity, there is, as Kung observed, a vital relationship between church and kingdom. In Christ, the reign of God has broken into the world in a decisive way and continues to be displayed in the church. In Colossians 1:12-13 for instance, there is clearly a close relationship between the *ekklesia* and the "kingdom of light" and the "kingdom of the Son."

Borrowing Kung's words again: "Even though it is not the kingdom of God which is to come, it is already under the reign of God which has begun"; the church anticipates the kingdom by being "its voice, its announcer, its herald."[3]

Thus we affirm that the church and the kingdom of God have a conspicuous and important relationship to one another, but they are not one and the same thing. The term "kingdom of God" denotes the kingly reign of God. It affirms divine sovereignty and points to the rule of God in someone's heart and life. By means of synonymous parallelism, a Hebrew literary device in which two lines constitute alternate ways of saying the same thing, Jesus defined it in the Model Prayer as the state of affairs that would exist when God's will is "done on earth as it is in heaven."

God adds all who are saved by the blood of Jesus Christ to the great fellowship known as the church. Then comes the real challenge. Can this saved woman allow God to reign over her pride and materialism? Can this redeemed man surrender his selfish ambition, foul temper, and hatred to

---

3. Ibid.

the sovereign rule of God? Will these church members pursue the kingdom of God in their daily experiences?

Recalling the word studies in Chapter Three, one keeps in mind that the word "church" essentially identifies an assembly. In Acts and the epistles, it is an assembly called together by God. For what purpose? To pursue the kingdom. Thus the church seeks to be an outpost of the divine reign in a world of rebels against God. It seeks to create an atmosphere where men and women can internalize and live the values of heaven.

As the church, then, we resist the arrogant claim that we embody the fullness of the kingdom of God. Yet we long for "a rich welcome into the eternal kingdom of our Lord and Savior Jesus Christ" (2 Pet. 1:11). Until then, we continue to pray, "Father, your kingdom come!" We commit ourselves to pursuing the kingdom lifestyle. We live the life of a pilgrim church moving toward a clearly identified goal.

Implications of a Pilgrim Status

As to the practical implications of this conception of the body of Christ as a pilgrim church, there are at least three that are important to this study in ecclesiology. Others may suggest themselves to you as you continue to reflect on the significance of this imagery.

First, the church's nature is best understood as movement toward an ideal, not the full embodiment of that ideal. If the church were to claim to be the complete realization of the kingdom, its claim would be idolatrous (i.e., claiming for itself what is the prerogative of deity) and appear hypocritical (i.e., since there is always a gap between the claim and the reality.)

The notion of a pilgrim church on the move toward the divine ideal not only helps avoid idolatry but also helps avoid complacency. Not being the finality of the kingdom does not grant the church the license to be indifferent about her shortcomings. To the contrary, the church must always seek the fuller reign of God in its experience. There is no room for resting on past achievements.

Consider two quite different approaches to the reading of church history. The first reading we will call the *Golden Age–Great Pit Theory* of church history, illustrated by the following diagram.

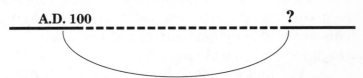

The dotted line represents the ideal church, the church in the mind of God in all of its glory and perfection. The solid line represents the church in its actual manifestation. According to this theory, the church of the New Testament corresponds perfectly to God's ideal. The church's "golden age" was lived out. As the apostolic age closed, though, the church deviated from the divine plan and plunged into the "great pit" of apostasy. At some later point in time—undoubtedly corresponding with the emergence of whatever religious tradition one wishes to champion—the church returns to its "golden age."

This approach to church history is both historically inaccurate and theologically dangerous. As we have already pointed out in earlier chapters, an original "golden age" is historical fiction. The church in its concrete existence has never fully embodied the ideal of God. The churches of the New Testament were racked by every type of sin still known among believers. Social, moral, and doctrinal problems were all there. Lamentable lack of commitment marked various early congregations. There has never been a perfect congregation, much less a time when the collective church in a given generation accomplished God's will with absolute fidelity.

It is also necessary to admit that no church today fully embodies that ideal. Just imagine someone pointing to a body of believers and saying, "This is the fleshly embodiment of God's will." The arrogance of such a claim is obvious.

But the fact that it is historically inaccurate is only part of the problem. What happens theologically when such an approach is taken? One claims ultimacy and perfection for human efforts at some particular point in history. There is a real sense in which, if the entire church was an altogether adequate "second incarnation," there would be little reason to continue to point back to the first. Why point to Jesus as the example of how God intends for man to live if one can point to a contemporary (or historical) church that equally embodies that ideal in fullness?

The second reading of church history we will call The Pilgrim Church Theory of church history. We can depict this approach with the following simple diagram:

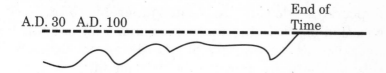

End of
A.D. 30   A.D. 100   Time

The dotted line again represents the ideal church, and the solid line is the church in its actual manifestations.

Notice first that the solid line and the dotted line never correspond until the end of time. They do not run together in the era of the New Testament church because, as discussed above, no church of that period fully embodied God's ideal. There is also no correspondence later in history with the emergence of any particular religious group. This does not mean, however, that there is no concrete example for the church to model. There is an exemplar and paradigm, but it is not a particular institutional form of the church in history. It is Jesus Christ himself. He is the dotted line in this diagram.

The wavering solid line indicates that there is a continuity in the history of the church from first century to middle ages to the present. The church generally, as well as particular congregations, has more closely or more distantly approximated God's ideal in Christ at various historical junctures. This is true of every era and region. This view is more

historically accurate and theologically sound. The
historical question has already been discussed, so
we can move on to theological matters.

This view claims ultimacy (i.e., all-sufficiency)
for Christ alone. It avoids both idolatry and
hypocrisy. It does not leave us vulnerable to the ac-
cusation of not living up to our claims, for our ultimate claims are only for our Lord and not for ourselves. We freely admit to being poor imitations of
our master. Nor, given this approach, are we
tempted to confuse the important distinctions in
the two incarnations. We dare not claim to be the
embodiment of God's heart and mind as Jesus was.

This approach also helps avoid complacency, because the pilgrim church is always striving to become what it is not yet. At the end of time, the
church will cease her striving and abide in perfect
union with her God, but not until then. If one believed that the church perfectly embodied God's
will in this life, why would one read the Bible since
there is nothing left to learn? Or why pray since
the relationship could not possibly be deepened?
The pilgrim church approach recognizes that the
task of becoming the people of God is never fully
accomplished but is a project worthy of a lifetime
commitment. We never rest contented on what we
have accomplished because there is still more to
come.

Incidentally (or perhaps not so incidentally) the
notion of the pilgrim church also leads to a different approach to church unity. Think about the radical difference in the two approaches depicted
below:

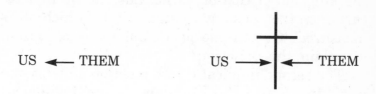

US ◄— THEM   US —►|◄— THEM

When a particular religious tradition believes that it lives so fully under the cross that it can move no closer to God's ideal as expressed in Jesus, the only approach to church unity its adherents can take is to call on everyone else to be just like them and thereby just like Jesus. Obviously when we call on the rest of the religious world to be just like us, they will be understandably suspicious. Must they change on everything while we need make no changes? There is little wonder that one religious tradition often views another as arrogant.

But maybe it is time for a brief moratorium on all such discussions. Perhaps before discussions between religious traditions can proceed with profit, we need a little more discussion within the particular religious heritages. Is it possible that we all need to spend a little time calling our own religious heritages back to Jesus Christ? If the church is a pilgrim church, this task must be reevaluated in every new generation. Just maybe, if each religious tradition would spend one generation trying to do nothing but be a more Jesus-like body, a generation from now inter-religious dialogue might take on a new tone.

Much is at stake with this first implication. Are we a pilgrim church or the ideal church? Are we the kingdom of God or its heralds? Is the first incarnation (i.e., Jesus) the standard by which all is measured? Or can one particular historical group also claim this privilege?

The second implication we mention only briefly: participation in the kingdom is the theological foundation for all of the church's activities. The church lives "between the times" of the decisive victory of the kingdom in the resurrection of Jesus and the consummation when "every knee shall bow." Between these times, the church proclaims the victory. Although the life and work of the church will be discussed in more detail later, it must be sufficient for now to point out that benevolence and evangelism and prophetic proclamation are all "kingdom" activities.

It is this participation in the kingdom that establishes the parameters of the church's activities. The church simply has no mandate for actions or programs that do not somehow contribute to the kingdom of God. When the church loses its way, it is often because it has forgotten its theological foundations. It is this theological foundation that sets the church apart. We will leave this point for further development in the chapter on the church's mission.

Third, the church is unable to bring the kingdom to consummation. This is a work that only God can accomplish. When one looks at the utopian passages from the Old Testament prophets that depict the reign of God, we begin to see how insufficient any human effort would be to bring it about.

In the last days
>the mountain of the Lord's temple will be
>>established
>>as chief among the mountains;
>it will be raised above the hills,
>>and peoples will stream to it.

Many nations will come and say,
>"Come, let us go up to the mountain of the
>>Lord,
>>to the house of the God of Jacob.
>He will teach us his ways,
>>so that we may walk in his paths."

The law will go out from Zion,
>the word of the Lord from Jerusalem.

He will judge between many peoples
>and will settle disputes for strong
>>nations far and wide.

They will beat their swords into plowshares
>and their spears into pruning hooks.

Nation will not take up sword against nation,
>nor will they train for war anymore.

Every man will sit under his own vine
>and under his own fig tree,

and no one will make them afraid,
>for the Lord Almighty has spoken,

All the nations may walk
>in the name of their gods;

We will walk in the name of the Lord
>our God for ever and ever (Mic. 4:1-5).

In the New Testament, the description of the final order of things (i.e., when God fully reigns) is also portrayed as beyond human effort and imagination.

Then I saw a new heaven and a new earth, for the first heaven and the first earth had passed away, and there was no longer any sea. I saw the Holy City, the new Jerusalem, coming down out of heaven from God, prepared as a bride beautifully dressed for her husband. And I heard a loud voice from the throne saying, "Now the dwelling of God is with men, and he will be with them. They will be his people, and God himself will be with them and be their God. He will wipe every tear from their eyes. There will be no more death or mourning or crying or pain, for the old order of things has passed away."

He who was seated on the throne said, "I am making everything new!" Then he said, "Write this down, for these words are trustworthy and true" (Rev. 21:1-5).

These beautifully poetic pictures point to the complete triumph of God that is discussed in the last chapter of this book. But it should be clear that this final victory is in the hands of God, not the church. This fundamental truth should bring both hope and humility to the pilgrim church.

It is a message of hope because the church is reassured that her final destiny is not dependent on her own fickle faith but on the absolute faithfulness of her God. Even the most cursory reading of church history serves to remind us of the dismal failures of the pilgrim church. Sometimes due to worldly resistance and the powers of darkness and at other times due to her own weakness and inadequacy, the church experiences periods of decline and ineffectiveness. But these are only temporary. The church confesses its shortcomings without being crushed by them, for the last word has yet to be given—and that word comes from God. The church lives with confidence in times of diminishment, for God will finish the task that he has begun. The reassuring words to the church in Philadelphia are ours as well: "I know that you have little strength, yet you have kept my word and have not denied my name. . . . I am coming soon. Hold on to what you have, so that no one will take your crown. Him who overcomes I will make a pillar in the temple of my God" (Rev. 3:8, 11).

But the fact that God completes the work should also humble the church. The church need not be smug about her triumphs because they are only partial and, in the final analysis, God's work after all. When we have done our best, we are still unprofitable servants. We have no reason to glory save in God's grace. So the church does not take undue pride in her victories or become overly depressed in her defeats. God's people simply go about the work of proclaiming the kingdom.

The bringing of the kingdom to consummation, then, must finally be a work of God. The church does not have the means to usher into the world the full reign of God. We need not despair, however; God will work his will in his own time. To herald this coming kingdom and to live under its shadow is presently all to which the church can aspire. But this is lofty enough work for the pilgrim church.

Conclusion

Knowing its destination rests in the hands of a faithful God who cannot be thwarted, the church goes patiently on its journey, attempting to draw ever nearer to the heart of God expressed in his son. The church is already experiencing a foretaste of the victory of the kingdom in her own life. It is imperfect but undaunted, ever praying: "Thy kingdom come, Thy will be done on earth as it is in heaven."

CHAPTER FIVE

Community:
The Fellowship of the Spirit

The world in which the Body of Christ must live is fragmented and disconnected. Relationships are often cold and formal. People tend to be increasingly competitive and frequently violent. Neighborhood ties are almost unknown; our mobility and urban sprawl—coupled with the fear of a knock on the door—have broken them. Marriage ties are not sacred. Children and parents are strangers to each other. And such symptoms of personal confusion as chemical dependency, divorce, and suicide confront us daily.

A sociologist has documented and described a phenomenon in American culture that he calls "ontological individualism."[1] By this term he identifies the belief that an individual is his own source of meaning. These rugged individualists see their world as so fragmented that they lack

1. Robert Bellah, *Habits of the Heart* (Berkeley: University of California Press, 1985).

even the vocabulary for expressing commitment or passion for anything other than themselves. His published research only confirms what we have all observed.

The Counter-Cultural Community

The church of the Lord Jesus Christ, however, is not founded on ontological individualism. If we import the spirit of our culture into the church, we will destroy one of its identifying marks. The church is *koinonia*, the fellowship of God's redeemed people. It is a spiritual family made up of diverse sisters and brothers. It is a colony of heaven planted on the earth. The church is a community that exists as a counter-culture to the world's splintered and hostile collection of individualists.

Beginning in the 1960s, we witnessed a public repudiation of the church in American religious life. "Jesus people" became prominent as spiritual individualists without social attachments or corporate life. From this root has grown a pseudo-theology that offers what one author has dubbed a "home correspondence course in salvation."

The New Testament vision of salvation permits no such church-bashing view of Christianity. While it is true that God saves individuals rather than groups, it is nevertheless also true that everyone he saves is immediately—and by the same process—incorporated into the Body of Christ. From the Pentecost Day when the church was founded until the second coming, those whom he saves he also adds to his church (Acts 2:47b).

In the words of Paul: "For we were all baptized by one Spirit into one body—whether Jews or Greeks, slave or free—and we were all given the one Spirit to drink" (1 Cor. 12:13). Notice also the metaphors from Peter that represent the believer as one within "a chosen people, a royal priesthood, a holy nation, a people belonging to God" (1 Pet. 2:9).

The Christian religion cannot be lived as a spiritual Lone Rangerism, for it is not a detached affair. Meditation in solitude may be the ultimate communion with God offered by some theological systems, but Christianity knows nothing of such a notion. The first and second commandments are necessarily joined to one another, and there is no love for and communion with God that is not also love for and communion with one another.

Though salvation is both personal and individual, it is not private. One who is born anew of water and Spirit is concurrently born into the family of God. He or she becomes a brother or sister to everyone else who has been spiritually reborn and becomes part of a community of faith. Christians are members of a larger family (Eph. 2:19), citizens within a new race or nation (1 Pet. 2:9), and building blocks within the Lord's holy temple (Eph. 2:21).

> Thus the very purpose of [Christ's] self-giving on the cross was not just to save isolated individuals, and so perpetuate their loneliness, but to create a new community whose members would belong to him, love one another, and eagerly serve the world.[2]

2. John R. W. Stott, *The Cross of Christ* (Downers Grove, IL: InterVarsity Press, 1986), p. 255.

The Body of Christ metaphor requires that we see every member in relationship not only to the head but with every other member. "The eye cannot say to the hand, 'I don't need you!'" and so on with all other members of the body (1 Cor. 12:21ff). To the contrary: "Now you are the body of Christ, and each one of you is a part of it" (1 Cor. 12:27). An individual apart from either the so-called invisible church or an identifiable local congregation is a form of Christian experience about which the New Testament knows nothing.

People need to belong, to be accepted, to fit in. Everyone needs to know that he or she is a significant member of a larger entity. Of all people, the church must be able to give this message to its members. "Those parts of the body that seem to be weaker are indispensable, and the parts that we think are less honorable we treat with special honor" (1 Cor. 12:22-23a). We have been accepted by God; we must accept one another. There must be no castes, no favoritism, and no discrimination. The church is Christ's spiritual body, and every member has a role to fill for the sake of its health and well-being.

The telephone in the church office rang one morning, and a sobbing lady was on the line. She was crying out for acceptance. Talking through her tears, with her voice becoming louder and more adamant, she said, "I don't want special attention. I don't want anyone to put a spotlight on me. I just want to be accepted!" Whether her isolation and sense of non-acceptance was her fault or someone else's is not the point; whether it was perceived or real is equally irrelevant here. We cite the episode only for the sake of emphasizing that everyone wants and needs acceptance. Part of the subjective assurance each of us needs that he or she has been accepted by God comes through the experience of being accepted within a spiritual fellowship that the New Testament calls the church.

Whatever else the church is supposed to be or do in the world, God has willed it to be a body of people in community. It is to present itself to God and men as a group of people banded together in partnership and sharing, in sympathy and mutual support. In their *Resident Aliens*, Hauerwas and Willimon have described the situation of those who are in Christ this way:

> For us, the world has ended. We may have thought that Jesus came to make nice people even nicer, that Jesus hoped to make a democratic Caesar just a bit more democratic, to make the world a bit better place for the poor. The Sermon [on the Mount], however, collides with such accommodationist thinking. It drives us back to a completely new conception of what it means for people to live with one another. That completely new conception is the church. All that we have heard said of old is thrown up for grabs, demands to be reexamined, and pushed back to square one. Square one is that colony made of those who are special, different, alien, and distinctive only in the sense that they are those who have heard Jesus say "Follow me," and have

come forth to be part of a new people, a
colony formed by hearing his invitation and
saying yes.[3]

The Church's *Koinonia*

The word used in the New Testament to name
the relationship among those who have responded
affirmatively to Christ's call is *koinonia*. Usually
translated "fellowship" in English Bibles, the term
comes from an important family of words signify-
ing sharing with someone or in something.[4] In a
passage from one of Plato's dialogues, there is a description of a dimly remembered time in early
Athens that makes a biblical student think immediately of Luke's account of the Jerusalem church:

> It was supplied with all that was required for
> its sustenance and training, and none of its
> members possessed any private property, but
> they regarded all they had as the *common
> property* (Gk, *koina*) of all; and from the rest
> of the citizens they claimed to receive nothing
> beyond a sufficiency of sustenance.[5]

In the New Testament, the *koinonia* of believers
was similarly presented in terms of an ideal society. It is not beyond imagining that such literate
men as Luke and Paul would have used this very
term to catch the attention of educated readers

3. Stanley Hauerwas and William H. Willimon, *Resident Aliens*
(Nashville: Abingdon Press, 1989), p. 92.
4. *Theological Dictionary of the New Testament*, 1965 ed., s.v.
"*koinos, koinonos, koinoneo, koinonia, synkoinonos, synkoinoneo,
koinonikos, koinoo*," by Freidrich Hauck.
5. Plato, *Critias* 110C-D; cf. Acts 4:32.

who knew the background of this word. Yet the New Testament *koinonia* was very different in its grounding from that envisioned by Plato and other Greek writers. It was not founded on the imitation of a past ideal or rooted in human initiative. It was grounded instead on a fellowship brought about by the Spirit of God. Thus the church is a visible, earthly society created by the redemptive work of Jesus. What Paul variously called "fellowship with his Son Jesus Christ our Lord" (1 Cor. 1:9), "the fellowship of the Holy Spirit" (2 Cor. 13:14), or "partnership in the gospel" (Phil. 1:5) points to a new relationship among humans that comes about because of divine intervention. The ideal for the community was never some dimly remembered Golden Age now past. The church knows its founder and head in history but is always forward—looking in hope. It is an eschatological fellowship.

Business relationships have partnerships. Classmates share. Fellow patients extend sympathy to each other. Players on the same football team support and encourage each other. But none of these relationships is the *koinonia* described in the New Testament and unique to Christians. Even if the participants in these situations were all Christians, their financial, educational, emotional, and athletic ties would not make these associations into churches.

Only those persons who have been placed as member-parts into the Body of Christ by the saving work of Christ are participants in heaven's community of men and women on earth. Such people may or may not be charming, pious, or desirable. They

may or may not have natural gifts and sympathies
that draw them to one another. But the creation of
a spiritual community is not determined by mutual
attractiveness-attractedness. Fellowship in Christ
is presented to us as a divine gift to *maintain*, not
held before us as an ideal to *attain*. Thus does
Bonhoeffer warn of

> the danger of confusing Christian brotherhood
> with some wishful idea of religious fellowship,
> of confounding the natural desire of the de-
> vout heart for community with the spiritual
> reality of Christian brotherhood. In Christian
> brotherhood everything depends upon its
> being clear right from the beginning, *first,*
> *that Christian brotherhood is not an ideal, but*
> *a divine reality. Second, that Christian broth-*
> *erhood is a spiritual and not a psychic*
> *reality.*[6]

His first point (i.e., "Christian brotherhood is
not an ideal, but a divine reality") is intended to
emphasize that one does not attain to fellowship in
the Body of Christ—which is bestowed along with
salvation—by working toward that goal; salvation
and membership in the community of the redeemed are gifts of grace through faith in Christ.
The second point (i.e., "Christian brotherhood is a
spiritual and not a psychic reality") affirms that
fellowship in Christ is neither the natural expression of homogeneity among the persons involved

---

6. Dietrich Bonhoeffer, *Life Together*, trans. by John W. Doberstein
(San Francisco: Harper & Row, 1954), p. 26. Italics in original.

nor the result of coercion by powerful personalities; it is the willingness to grant that Jesus alone is our unity and to see one another through his eyes.

The lived experience of Christian fellowship, as opposed to all other types of human community, may be defined then as *one's active involvement with another child of God so as to encourage his or her growth in spiritual things*. This definition entails at least three significant elements.

First, it involves the recognition of an individual as a fellow believer in Christ (i.e., a Christian). All those who are God's children by virtue of a new birth of water and the Spirit are brothers and sisters to one another. They have been brought from darkness to light and have a new relationship with one another based on the forgiveness of sin. Paul attributed the unity of Jew and Greek, slave and free, male and female to the following: "You are all sons of God through faith in Christ Jesus, for all of you who were united with Christ in baptism have been clothed with Christ" (Gal. 3:26-27).

The "right hand of fellowship" given to Paul and Barnabas (Gal. 2:9) was no mere handshake but a public recognition of these men as brothers in the Lord by such pillar Christians as Peter and James the brother of Jesus. More than that, it was an endorsement of their ministry of preaching the gospel to the Gentiles by Christians of Hebrew ethnic background.

People within the community of Christ often function and relate within it on the basis of common interests that are not distinctively Christian. Churches even foster this approach by creating programs that are sociologically viable but theologically monstrous. Exercise groups, child-care classes, and athletic teams are neither inappropriate to a Christian lifestyle nor improper offerings for a church. But it is not merely involvement with other Christians but a critical focus on Christ that sets Christian fellowship apart from all others. With a given convert to Christ, the church's goal must be more than social integration. We must seek to ground a relationship with him or her which, while perhaps including Thursday night softball games, is genuinely spiritual in nature.

Second, the definition offered above holds that Christian community requires "active involvement" with fellow believers. It is a positive rather than negative relationship, thus it must show itself in active rather than passive ways. Fellowship can never be mere tolerance and avoidance of doing harm. It implies observing, caring, and acting in positive ways. Delivered from the self-centeredness of their sinful natures, redeemed people are capable of seeking the welfare of others. "Each of you should look not only to your own interests, but also to the interests of others" (Phil. 2:4).

Mere words without deeds that implement their sentiment will not count as spiritual fellowship. Thus believers are exhorted: "Dear children, let us not love with words or tongue but with actions and in truth" (1 John 3:18). The Johannine epistle just quoted proceeds to expand on this theme by rooting a Christian understanding of a loving community in the perfect example of divine love. "Dear friends, let us love one another, for love comes from God," writes the apostle. "Everyone who loves has been born of God and knows God" (1 John 4:7). This exposition of Christian fellowship ends with a bold challenge-rebuke: "If anyone says, 'I love God,' yet hates his brother, he is a liar. For anyone who does not love his brother, whom he has seen, cannot love God, whom he has not seen. And he has given us this command. Whoever loves God must also love his brother" (1 John 4:20-21).

The early church's sharing of goods (Acts 4:32ff) was the fellowship of active involvement. So was the encouragement of Paul's evangelistic mission among the Gentiles by believers in Jerusalem. Brotherly love shows itself in practical and creative ways wherever it exists.

Third, Christian fellowship is a means of encouraging another's growth in spiritual things. Paul was bolstered in times of stress by the gifts sent him by the church at Philippi (Phil. 4:14-19). All Christians are urged to bear each other's burdens (Gal. 6:2), extend hospitality (Heb. 13:1-2), and "do what leads to peace and mutual edification" (Rom. 14:19).

The objective truth of a *koinonia* bestowed on Christians as a gift of grace becomes observationally real in a variety of ways: shared worship experiences (whether public or private), pooling funds for good works, giving and receiving counsel, weeping, laughing, eating together, etc. While believers may perform many of these same actions (e.g., eating) with unbelievers, such acts shared among Christians constitute implicit expressions of spiritual involvement and concern because they see each other through the eyes of Christ.

Fellowship, then, is a deliberate sharing and joint participation in the spiritual lives of others in love. It is predicated on the prior experience of each believer in being united with God through Jesus Christ. It is the experience of being a spiritual family by virtue of common paternity. The objective fact of fraternity has become the basis for experiences that demonstrate the practical meaning of community.

One can summarize all this by saying that the church is a *community* by virtue of its *commonalities*. A common threat (sin) has been met by a common salvation (Christ's atoning death) for the sake of imparting a common gift (eternal life) that manifests itself in a common distinctiveness (Christ-like character). One has access to membership in this community by a common rite of entrance (baptism) and is empowered to function within it by a common agent (the Holy Spirit). Salvation is celebrated regularly within the fellowship by a common ceremony (the Lord's Supper). Everyone in this colony of faith has a common purpose for life (the glory of God) and a common aspiration for the life to come (sharing God's fellowship in heaven).

Since only God knows the full truth about any one of us, it is certainly possible for us to err in giving or withholding our spiritual participation in the lives of others. On the one hand, it would be possible to extend fellowship to someone who is in fact still outside of Christ. On the other hand, it would also be possible to deny fellowship to someone the Lord has accepted. Divine judgment is according to the full truth; on the other hand, we are always limited by partial knowledge and errors in judgment.

Within any church, spiritual babes, those who fall into sin, and any who hold unorthodox views—and these three categories surely include us all!—are to be held within the fellowship for the sake of nurturing them, teaching them, and salvaging them.

The extreme step of expelling someone from the church's fellowship ought to occur only in three cases: when a doctrinal error that person embraces negates the very heart of the gospel message (2 John 7-9; cf. 1 John 2:18-23), when sinful behavior is flagrant and persistent (1 Cor. 5:1-11), or when a divisive spirit is exhibited that runs roughshod over others and violates their freedom in Christ (3 John 9-10; Tit. 3:10-11). Even in these severe cases, however, the threat of excommunication or disfellowship may carry little weight because of the lack of any prior experience of real community that was meaningful to the individual in question. This fact alone alerts us to a deficiency that should frighten us.

A Utopian Vision?

Literature is replete with attempts to describe what have come to be called *utopian* communities. Plato's *Republic* is probably the oldest and best known of this genre; it describes an ideal state ruled by philosopher-kings. Sir Thomas More wrote his *Utopia* in the sixteenth century to picture his own version of such a place. And various attempts at establishing such communities have been tried—most of them being short-lived experiments that ended in frustration and cynicism. Against these human experiments with social experience, the church stands as a divine reality.

Against the nowhere (i.e., the meaning of the Greek term from which "utopia" derives) of an ideal society, the church exists everywhere the Word of God goes as a counter-culture of the kingdom of heaven. Its existence does not depend on a certain governmental structure, economic arrangement, or level of literacy. With people "from every tribe and language and people and nation," Jesus Christ continually creates "a kingdom and priests to serve our God" (Rev. 5:9-10). This priestly kingdom has as its distinctive mark the sovereign reign of God in the hearts and lives of those who know Christ as Lord. In whatever part of the world and under whatever form of human government, these people live as a colony of heaven (cf. Phil. 3:20).

These people are not formed into a community through the human pursuit of fraternity but through shared spiritual unity with Jesus. Their fellowship is a goal being achieved through the divine process of salvation. Men and women were created for fellowship with God, and sin disrupted that fellowship—both with him and with one another. Redemption from sin has taken away the barrier between them and God, and ongoing spiritual growth is removing barriers among themselves. They are being made one by the power of the one Spirit who indwells them all in order both to validate and to empower their unique experience.

Unlike Plato's ideal state or More's theoretical society, Christ's church is a reality. Oh, it is not a fully established kingdom yet; it is still in the process of forming. It exists now only in its partial form as a "pilgrim church" striving for an ideal identity. Yet it does exist as a beginning, an always-in-jeopardy outpost of heaven within a hostile environment.

The reason so many texts about the kingdom of God confuse us is that the kingdom is both realized and anticipated. Like our salvation, which is both a present possession and a longed-for goal, so is the kingdom both present and future. To the degree that we allow the reign of God in our lives and constitute an alternative to the world, we experience the kingdom now; to the degree that we desire a perfect sovereignty for our God, we know that the present world situation is antagonistic toward him and that "in keeping with his promise we are looking forward to a new heaven and a new earth, the home of righteousness" (2 Pet. 3:13).

What the community of saved people called the church is doing "between the times" is eternally significant. Its presence in the world bears witness to the cross. In all circumstances, it testifies to a view of reality that takes eternity more seriously than time. As a visible community of faith, it is called of God to bear witness to life in the midst of death, truth in the midst of lies, joy in the midst of despair, and good in the midst of evil.

When trying to understand the meaning of Christian community in relation to the surrounding world, one could go to sources much less reliable than a second-century document written as a defense of the faith.

Christians cannot be distinguished from the rest of the human race by country or language or customs. They do not live in cities of their own; they do not use a peculiar form of speech; they do not follow an eccentric manner of life. This doctrine of theirs has not been discovered by the ingenuity or deep thought of inquisitive men, nor do they put forward a merely human teaching, as some do. Yet, although they live in Greek and barbarian cities alike, as each man's lot has been cast, and follow the customs of the country in clothing and food and other matters of daily living, at the same time they give proof of the remarkable and admittedly extraordinary constitution of their own commonwealth.

They live in their own countries, but only as aliens. They have a share in everything as citizens, and endure everything as foreigners. Every foreign land is their fatherland, and yet for them every fatherland is a foreign land.

They marry, like everyone else, and they beget children, but they do not cast out their offspring. They share their board with each other, but not their marriage bed. It is true that they are "in the flesh," but they do not live "according to the flesh."

They busy themselves on earth, but their citizenship is in heaven. They obey the established laws, but in their own lives they go far beyond what the laws require. They love all men, and by all men are persecuted. They are unknown, and still they are condemned; they are put to death, and yet they are brought to life. They are poor, and yet they make many rich; they are completely destitute, and yet they enjoy complete abundance. They are dishonored, and in their very dishonor are glorified; they are defamed, and are vindicated.

They are reviled, and yet they bless; when they are affronted, they still pay due respect. When they do good, they are punished as evil-doers; undergoing punishment, they rejoice because they are brought to life. They are treated by the Jews as foreigners and enemies, and are hunted down by the Greeks; and all the time those who hate them find it impossible to justify their enmity.

To put it simply: What the soul is in the body, that Christians are in the world.[7]

The distinctive calling of the church in any age is not to "let the world set the agenda" for its activities nor to adopt the spirit of the time. The church must simply be the church. It must be a redemptive and healing community for its own members; it must be conscience and counter-culture for the world.

How It Works

What does this community of faith called *the church* look like? Where is (or has been) its perfect instantiation? What prototype of it can we fasten on for the sake of imitation?

---

7. *Letter to Diognetus* 5:1—6:1.

There is no perfect example of it—either in the biblical record, in church history, or today. Such a fellowship is always forming yet never perfected among God's people. Returning to last chapter's discussion of the nature of the church, we are still praying for the kingdom to come.

Often naively pictured as the happy, unintended result of simply being together, *koinonia* is the deliberate breaking down of barriers between God and his human creatures which is ongoing in the process known as salvation. But how do we break down the barriers? How do we reach to each other and live as a redemptive and healing community? How shall we achieve the goal of being both conscience and counter-culture to the world?

First, we must resist the current trend toward isolation in our culture. The difficulty Americans have making commitments to others, whether in marriages, voluntary organizations, or political entities, has been documented by researchers such as Robert Bellah. The church cannot exist as a scattered flock; Christ has gathered us together. We must experience and celebrate our sense of belonging to one another in Christ's body with assemblies. We need to get together in the sorts of all-church worship experiences we know but sometimes treat with a spirit ranging from indifference to contempt. As the unnamed writer of Hebrews anticipated a crisis of major proportions for believers, he said: "Let us not give up meeting together, as some are in the habit of doing, but let us encourage one another—and all the more as you see the Day approaching" (Heb. 10:25).

Second, we must allow the Spirit of God to quicken our assemblies with freshness and life. Our assemblies need not be dull exercises in boring ritual. They can be creative, alive, and refreshing to the spirit. In order to be worthy of our God and in order to convince people that he is present in them, this sort of vibrancy must be sensed.

We are not talking about manipulating feelings in order to create tawdry imitations of spiritual encounter. To the contrary, we are proposing that the community of faith recapture its zeal for God that shows itself in worship. More will be said on this in a later chapter.

Third, we must make close contact with each other, form burden-bearing and joy-sharing personal relationships, and communicate both the content and passion of our faith with one another. This cannot happen in all-church assemblies. It requires one-on-one and small-group experiences where spiritual intimacy can be experienced.

The success of such 12-step programs as Alcoholics Anonymous has been discussed in many forms over the past decade. In the context of acceptance and confidentiality, people are allowed to bare their souls. Addictions, infidelities, and criminal behaviors are detailed to one another. There is a strange mixture of laughter and tears as participants recognize themselves in one another. People abandon defensiveness and become vulnerable to one another. And they do all this without condemnation of each other. They are all in it together, know the pain of self-judgment, and want to find a beginning point for the hope of recovery.

These "secular" meetings that are held by the millions across the United States had to be created because the church had failed. Although this approach is founded on a biblical model,[8] churches had typically become too stiff and formal to allow something so "radical." While these non-church groups are helping untold numbers of people deal with problems through mutual confession, personal involvement, and support during difficult times, their ability is limited. A vague "Higher Power" coupled with "searching moral inventory" falls far short of the forgiveness that comes only through Jesus Christ when one repents and believes the gospel.

Many churches have begun creating small-group Bible studies after the 12-step paradigm. What a shame that the biblical model of *koinonia* is having to be learned from the outside. But thank God it is being used again!

The caution must be sounded, however, against baptizing a secular model with Christian nomenclature. Merely calling it a "Life Group" or "Bible Study Group" will not make it a time and place of spiritual fellowship. The authority of Scripture must be kept above the authority of group senti-

---

8. The initial platform of what would become Alcoholics Anonymous was derived from a spiritual movement initially known as the First Century Christian Fellowship and later as the Oxford Group. Founded by an ordained Lutheran minister, it advocated "four absolutes" (i.e., absolute honesty, absolute purity, absolute unselfishness, and absolute love) and also "getting square with God." Cf. Nan Robertson, *Getting Better: Inside Alcoholics Anonymous* (New York: William Morrow and Company, Inc., 1988), pp. 56-85.

ment. The group must seek God rather than self-expression and, while avoiding judgment of one another, sit collectively under the judgment of God. With Christ as the goal, the Bible must be accepted as the final source of truth and direction for living.

In our city's morning newspaper, a letter to the editor provided an insight into the impact that churches could have on the world if they were seen as close-knit communities of love and support. A woman told of having a late dinner in a local restaurant with her two children. Halfway through their meal, the place began to fill up with what first appeared to be a family reunion. Each person or small group entering was greeted and hugged by the larger group. There was warmth and genuine interest. Phrases like "Call me if you need to talk" and "I love you" were heard again and again. Before leaving, the mother asked about the nature of the age-integrated, actively networking, happy meeting. Someone told her it was a group that gathered every Saturday night to follow up their Alcoholics Anonymous meeting. The woman's 13-year-old son then asked, "Do you have to be an alcoholic to join?"[9]

Where can people find help to confront their problems? Where do they find friends when lonely, encouragement when in despair, help when unemployed? Is there a club or support group somewhere for *everyone*?

God founded it a long time ago. The New Testament calls it the church, the Body of Christ,

9. (Nashville) *Tennessean*, 4 October 1989, p. 8A.

the Family of God. It is Everyman's fellowship for males and females, slaves and free, Jews and Gentiles, blacks and whites, alcoholics and teetotalers—anyone who seeks divine guidance, strength, and support.

First-century believers were together frequently. They not only met together as the church but in one another's homes. Their corporate life focused on praise to God and spiritual encouragement for one another. No wonder outsiders saw what was happening among them and wanted to be part of it. Perhaps today's churches need to rediscover what many seem to have lost and AA appears to have found. The boy watching the restaurant group was impressed enough that he wanted to know about joining Alcoholics Anonymous after only one contact. When that begins to happen with churches, we will have recaptured something we never should have lost.

Perhaps it would not be incorrect to say that AA still preserves the essence of entering into fellowship—*sharing our stories*. What bonds a 65-year-old black man, a 27-year-old white girl, and a 43-year-old Hispanic in a functioning 12-step group? Each finds himself or herself in the story being told by the others. A bond is forged that blends heightened self-awareness with sensitive other-awareness.

Christians are one by virtue of a shared story of salvation. Each finds himself in the other's report of salvation. Each sees his or her own story linked to the Christ-event. In this sharing of personal narrative and Word of God, people discover one another as brothers and sisters in the family of God.

Conclusion

In the community that is Christ's church, walls come down. "There is neither Jew nor Greek, slave nor free, male nor female, for you are all one in Christ" (Gal. 3:28). The fragmented and disconnected world described in the opening paragraph of this chapter gives way to the *koinonia* of Christ's spiritual body.

In a healthy church, Christ shows his people the meaning of accepting one another, esteeming one another, and loving one another. Because he has received them, they receive one another. Because the church provides a unique framework of loving support for recovering sinners (e.g., fornicators, drunks, preachers, liars, hypocrites, deacons, gossips, etc.), it is irreplaceable in their lives. They attend its assemblies. They finance its ministries. They sacrifice time to be involved in its work.

Christ purchased the church with his own blood (Acts 20:28). His truth guides its actions. His Spirit fills and animates its work. His living presence is experienced in its fellowship. Anyone who has never been part of such a community cannot understand the church's *koinonia*.

The church is a spiritual body whose very nature ends alienation, breaks down walls, and provides support for spiritual healing. As fidelity to the head increases, our community with one another will become more evident. The doctrine of an incorporeal "invisible church" will be supplemented by a more believable and accessible "visible church" that exists as an alternative community to a society eroded of corporate identity by self-centeredness.

In order for such a visible expression of Christ's presence in community to exist, those of us who are in the church must recapture biblical thinking. We are not a mere collection of saved individuals but a fellowship of interactive personalities. Our goal is not merely to develop personal spirituality but to become a community of the Spirit of God.

Fellowship, then, is not necessarily related to the amount of time people spend together; in a given day's duty, one may spend more time with associates, colleagues, and fellow laborers with whom there is no spiritual community than with those to whose souls that person is bound by an unbreakable bond. Neither is it a social phenomenon to be judged by frequency of contact or shared events; one's most intimate comrades may be seen only occasionally, but they will always be seen through fraternal eyes.

The active agent who creates such a fellowship is the Holy Spirit. A single Spirit indwelling every member of the Body of Christ draws us together. Yet he does not accomplish his work of creating community against our wills. We must submit our wills to his purpose and, following the explicit teachings of Jesus and his example with his disciples, be willing to find each other in our shared story of redemption in Christ.

"Don't you know that you yourselves are God's temple and that God's Spirit lives in you? If anyone destroys God's temple, God will destroy him; for God's temple is sacred, and you are that temple" (1 Cor. 3:16-17).

Fundamental
Relations

CHAPTER SIX

Worship:
The Church Relates To God

The late A. W. Tozer wrote:

> For whatever we can say of modern Bible-
> believing Christians, it can hardly be denied
> that we are not remarkable for our spirit of
> worship. The gospel as preached by good men
> in our times may save souls, but it does not
> create worshipers.
>
> Our meetings are characterized by cordial-
> ity, humor, affability, zeal and high animal
> spirits; but hardly anywhere do we find gath-
> erings marked by the overshadowing presence
> of God. We manage to get along on correct
> doctrine, fast tunes, pleasing personalities
> and religious amusements. . . .
>
> If Bible Christianity is to survive the pre-
> sent world upheaval, we shall need to recap-

ture the spirit of worship. We shall need to
have a fresh revelation of the greatness of
God and the beauty of Jesus. We shall need to
put away our phobias and our prejudices
against the deeper life and seek again to be
filled with the Holy Spirit. He alone can raise
our cold hearts to recapture and restore again
the art of true worship.[1]

How correct was his observation? What has
changed since he made it? Is the challenge to "recapture the spirit of worship" sensed by this generation? If sensed, is the challenge being met?

Hardly any subject receives more discussion
than worship when the issue at hand is the
church's impact (or lack of impact) on the world.
Much of what is said is negative and focuses on the
disinterest of non-Christians in the corporate event
churches call "worship assemblies." Even those
who participate in (or, perhaps, merely *attend*)
these convocations do so with a sense of hesitancy
because of what they label the "boring" or "irrelevant" character of what happens in them.

Young people sometimes complain about the archaic language and dull music of the church's
hymns. Introduce a piece of contemporary
Christian music for the younger members of the
congregation, though, and some older members
may rise up in protest. Must there be two churches
with different musical tastes?

---

1. A. W. Tozer, "The Art of True Worship," *That Incredible
Christian* (Harrisburg, PA: Christian Publications, Inc., 1964), pp.
130-131.

Every ingredient of worship seems to generate some element of contention among those who are called to share in it. Surely this is not novel to our generation. Perhaps there is no resolution to the problem.

At the very least, however, we should make an effort to understand more about worship than most of us seem to comprehend. Most Christians appear to have nothing that resembles a *"theology* of worship" to guide them through the resolution of questions concerning it. Recapturing what Tozer called the *"spirit* of worship" awaits both theological and personal grappling with the issue.

Two Misleading Theses

Much of our uncertainty about worship in today's context stems from two mistaken points of view. In order to arrive at something positive, it will first be necessary to take a negative look at those theses.

First, a widely held view these days seems to be that *all of life is worship.* Historically, this position likely arose as a corrective against a static view that saw New Testament worship as a competitive alternative to Old Testament ritual. In other words, one pattern or system was being replaced by a new one. The critical element, then, was to identify and correctly perform the "acts of worship" appropriate to the New Testament church.

There are some conspicuous differences between Hebrew and Christian worship. A fundamental one is the concept of priesthood. Unlike the Old Testament model in which only a select body of priests could come before Yahweh with sacrifices and offerings as worship, the New Testament invites every believer to see himself or herself as a priest before the Lord. Christ alone fills the role of the priest who offers the sacrifice of atonement. He has gained entrance into the heavenly temple and has presented his blood as the perfect and final atonement for sin. The altar is therefore conspicuous for its absence in Christian assemblies. Christ's once-for-all sacrifice of himself has rendered it unnecessary and inappropriate.

This much of the claim "all of life is worship" is correct: Our worship is not confined to a particular time or place. The ancient debate about worship at Gerazim versus Jerusalem has been rendered meaningless (cf. John 4:21-24). Praise and thanksgiving are not limited to a few holy places on a select number of holy days. They are the rule of life for Christians under all circumstances. Thus Paul can urge his readers "to offer your bodies as living sacrifices, holy and pleasing to God—this is your spiritual act of worship" (Rom. 12:1).

Yet it should also be pointed out that Paul's emphasis is not unique to the New Testament. Even Old Testament prophets said that ritual activity alone (i.e., divorced from life) was insufficient. "With what shall I come before the LORD?" was Micah's question in the eighth century B.C. As its answer, he considered burnt offerings, calves, and "thousands of rams." Rejecting these commanded sacrifices as adequate for one who would worship Yahweh, he concluded instead that God's demand was broader than some had come to interpret it.

Ritual without godliness would be meaningless, so his final answer to the question came in this form: "He has showed you, O man, what is good. And what does the LORD require of you? To act justly and to love mercy and to walk humbly with your God" (Mic. 6:8).

This is not to say that good living makes traditional worship activities unnecessary. In the biblical texts just cited, the warning is against using ritual as a substitute for ethics. We can imagine contemporary settings where the prophetic word would be used in another way—against the contrary tendency to substitute Christian ethics for what we commonly think of as worship. Thus a person who has treated customers and employees fairly from Monday through Friday decides to spend a recreational weekend at the lake with no remorse over a failure to assemble with other saints for corporate worship on the Lord's Day.

The word translated "worship" in Romans 12:1 is *latreia*. It is a term used several times in the Septuagint, typically to describe the sacrifice-based worship of Israel's experience. In all five of its New Testament occurrences, the idea of sacrifice is constantly present. In his metaphorical use of the term in this text, Paul applies it to the homage paid God when Christians offer themselves to God in daily dedication, discipleship, and devotion.

> Christian worship does not consist of what is practiced at sacred sites, at sacred times, and with sacred acts (Schlatter). It is the offering of bodily existence in the otherwise profane

sphere. As something constantly demanded
this takes place in daily life, whereby every
Christian is simultaneously sacrifice and
priest.[2]

This much granted, however, there is more to be
said about Christian worship. To take this important truth about Christian life as the totality of a
theology of worship would be a serious mistake. It
is to ignore the practical reality that one is unlikely
to focus intently on God or consciously articulate
his praise while checking last week's inventory list.
Effectual worship is much more likely to occur in a
place of private devotion or in an assembly with
other determined worshipers when a block of time
is intentionally set aside to seek the face of God.

At its heart, worship is the reply of the creature
to the Creator. It is the response of the beloved to
the Lover. It is the reaction of the ransomed to the
Redeemer. Worship is an experience of deliberate
focusing on God for the purpose of encounter with
him.

Plato observed that the idea of God is too big for
the human mind to wrap around. Precisely! And
thus is born the attitude from which worship
springs. When one becomes aware of a God who is
more than the conclusion to a theistic argument,
greater than anything the human understanding
can approach, and too magnificent to explain, he

---

2. Ernst Kasemann, *Commentary on Romans*, translated and
edited by Geoffrey W. Bromiley (Grand Rapids: William B.
Eerdmans Publishing Company, 1982), p. 329; cf. Strathmann, *"la-
treuo, latreia,"* in *Theological Dictionary of the New Testament*, 4:
58-65.

bows low before that God and whispers, "Holy!" Or he dances before him and shouts, "Holy!" Or he weeps before him and cries, "Holy!" Or he is too struck with awe to say anything at all.

Worship reaches its practical climax with the internalization of the sacrifice motif that moves the worshiper to offer himself or herself as a living sacrifice to God, but it always has personal encounter with God as its essence. To encounter God, though, is to be overwhelmed by his holiness and judgment, by his grace and forgiveness, by his sovereignty and love. These experiences of confrontation force us to bow down and worship. Whether by a well in Mesopotamia, where one man "bowed down and worshiped" (Gen. 24:26), or around the heavenly throne, where the four living creatures and the 24 elders "fell down and worshiped" (Rev. 5:14), encountering God produces the awareness of his awesome presence which can only be acknowledged with worship. When one catches a glimpse of God, worship is spontaneous and unavoidable. It is the most natural response the human heart can make to the awareness of deity.

Second, what has been said to this point challenges another common thesis of our time that *the Christian experience of worship is principally intended for edification.* The church is seriously debilitated when worship is taken to be a group-directed project rather than a God-directed event. It is tempting in such a context to accommodate an entertainment model that proposes to satisfy the customers rather than exalt God.

While there is a strong element of edification accompanying true worship (cf. 1 Cor. 14:26), focus on God in his own person rather than the edification of his devotees must be at the heart of the worship experience. But is the term "worship experience" misleading in itself? Some think so and object to it because it suggests that worship is important by reason of the feelings it can produce in participants. Whether the term itself is objectionable, we leave to the taste of each reader; the notion of reducing worship to warm and pleasing feelings called forth in participants is simply wrong-headed. Though worship frequently generates good experiences and leaves one with pleasant feelings, neither the experience nor the attendant feeling is correctly termed worship. That many are unable to make this distinction is evidenced by the fact that they are quick to judge the entertainment value of a church service while remaining unfamiliar with the reality to which it can open us. It is one thing to say—as Scripture does—that a by-product of worship is edification; it is quite another thing to say that the essence of worship is edification.

Job's worship of the Lord was anything but an aesthetic experience that left him with good feelings. And so with much of the worship reflected in the Psalms and other sections of Holy Scripture. We are probably most worshipful when we are the least conscious of the worship itself. To say the least, when worship becomes self-conscious rather than God-conscious, its purpose has been defeated. Mere tinkering with the sequence of events, tempo of the music, or length of the sermon makes no substantial difference in worship. Only when an encounter with the Living God is fostered—with whatever "feelings" may accompany that encounter (e.g., celebration, melancholy, tears, laughter, judgment, etc.)—has worship transpired.

To create settings that deliberately manipulate emotions and tantalize participants is cheap theater rather than worship. Or, if one insists on calling it worship, it is self-worship rather than the worship of God. True worship does not call attention to itself; it serves instead as a means for focusing attention on God. As with any spiritual sign, worship points to a greater reality that lies behind the immediate experience. It points beyond itself to the Living God who is the object of worship.

The Nature of Worship

Our English term *worship* traces to the Anglo-Saxon "worth-ship." It means to attribute worth to an object or person. Thus one might say of a materialistic person that "He worships his money" or "She worships her jewels." A title such as "His Worship the Mayor" indicates that, for certain purposes at least, a designated individual is the most significant person in the city's population. This concept of worship as adoration and awe is not merely a reflection of our English term but is also true to the worship vocabulary of Scripture.

There are two pivotal Hebrew verbs that define the attitude appropriate to worship. There is `abad which means "to serve." It originally pointed to physical work a slave might perform for his owner-master but came to be used for activities of worship, whether to the true God or to pagan idols. This word is used in Yahweh's communication to Moses at Horeb: "When you have brought the people out of Egypt, you will *worship* God on this mountain" (Ex. 3:12b; cf. 4:23; 7:16; 8:1, *et al.*).

Then there is *histah*^a*wah* which means "to bow down" in reverence and humility before another, whether man or God. Thus when Abraham received the three strangers, "he hurried from the entrance of his tent to meet them and *bowed* low to the ground" (Gen. 18:2). And David could anticipate a time when "all the families of the nations will *bow down* before" Yahweh (Psa. 22:27).

While both of these words suggest physical action, it is proper to observe that both look beyond mere bodily ritual to the obedient service which comes from a bowing of one's will to God in sincerity. Thus the former term is found at Deuteronomy 10:12-13 ("And now, O Israel, what does the LORD your God ask of you but to fear the LORD your God, to walk in all his ways, to love him, *to serve* the LORD your God with all your heart and with all your soul, and to observe the LORD'S commands and decrees that I am giving you today for your own good?") and the latter in Exodus 12:27-28 ("Then the people *bowed down* and worshiped. The Israelites did just what the Lord commanded Moses and Aaron").

Moving now to the New Testament, five Greek terms are especially significant with regard to worship. *Proskyneo* is a verb found 59 times from Matthew to Revelation. Its original meaning was probably "to kiss" and came to signify prostrating oneself (perhaps to kiss the ground) before the Holy God. It always denotes reverence shown to one who is superior (cf. Matt. 4:9-10; Acts 10:25-26; Rev. 14:7).

The *gonypeteo* ("to bend the knee") word group in the New Testament points to an attitude of respect and adoration that shows itself in a physical gesture. Therefore one may kneel to pray (Luke 22:41), to make a petition of Jesus (Matt. 17:14), or to acknowledge Christ as Lord of all (Phil. 2:10).

Another important word group found in the New Testament involves *latreuo/latreia*. It traces back to a secular word for wages and likely slipped into Greek religious vocabulary in connection with the idea of paying one his due. The words mean "to serve/service" and signify that God is due to receive the devoted service of his creatures. The verb occurs 21 times in the New Testament and the noun five times. As pointed out earlier in this chapter, this word group can refer either to formal events of worship (Heb. 8:5; 12:22) or to the service one renders to God in the daily events of his life (Rom. 12:1; cf. John 16:2).

The noun *threskeia* is also found in the New Testament and refers to the "service of God" (Acts 26:5; Jas. 1:26b-27). Its adjectival form, *threskos*, means "pious, religious" (Jas. 1:26a). There is little difference in meaning from *latreia*.

Finally there is *leitourgeo*. This verb means "to serve" and occurs only three times in the New Testament; the related nouns *leitourgia* (service) and *leitourgos* (servant) are found six and five times respectively. While they may refer to a community's worship rituals (Phil. 2:17; Heb. 8:2), these words are sometimes practical equivalents to the *diakoneo/diakonos* word group (Phil. 2:25, 30).

From this survey of vocabulary words for worship, one infers that to worship God is to exalt him as the one above all others, to assign supreme worth to him. Yet that experience is somehow understood as having implications for daily behavior that shows itself in service to God and to the community of his people. Strange as it may sound to someone who has not experienced it, worship that affirms the glory of God, encounters him in his righteousness, and shares in his grace places all things of this world in their proper place and makes it possible to live the rest of one's existence as a living sacrifice to God. True worship allows one to see herself and the issues of her life in light of the sacred presence of God. It releases him from the idol of self and liberates his heart from the gods of the marketplace. It frees one from self-centeredness and frees him to serve the needs of others.

In theological language, worship is the creature's acknowledgment of the Creator's transcendence. Or, as one writer has expressed it: "Worship is the dramatic celebration of God in his supreme worth in such a manner that his 'worthiness' becomes the norm and inspiration of human living."[3]

It is also true, however, that worship relates directly to daily life and principled behavior. It is not merely that in worship contexts we are frequently exhorted to our moral duties. It is rather that wor-

---

3. Ralph P. Martin, *The Worship of God* (Grand Rapids: William B. Eerdmans Publishing Co., 1982), p. 4.

ship itself lifts us to an experience of God that transforms his worshipers.

> To be sure, worship can be used as a nar-
> cotic trip into another world to escape the eth-
> ical responsibilities of living a Christian life
> in this world. Religious rituals easily lend
> themselves to corruption. . . . The prophets re-
> mind us that our rituals can become a retreat
> from reality, crude attempts to compensate for
> our moral misdeeds through cultic deeds, and
> a means of avoiding the ethical cost of disci-
> pleship through the ersatz discipleship of the
> cult.[4]

These reflections on worship point to a direct correlation between two items which nowadays seem to be incompatible in the minds of many: *reverence* and *relevance*. The prevailing notion seems to be that one must choose between the two. Reverence is "high church," archaic, and unrelated to life; relevance is "low church," trendy, and in touch with current issues.

Isaiah 6: God-Directed Worship

In defense of the explanations already offered and in an effort to dispel the myth that reverence and relevance are antithetical aspects of worship, think back to the Lord's commission of Isaiah. It constitutes something of a paradigm for God-directed worship that has immediate application to life.

---

4. William Willimon, *The Service of God* (Nashville: Abingdon Press, 1983), pp. 41-42.

In the year that King Uzziah died, I saw the Lord seated on a throne, high and exalted, and the train of his robe filled the temple. Above him were seraphs, each with six wings: With two wings they covered their faces, with two they ccvered their feet, and with two they were flying. And they were calling to one another:

"Holy, holy, holy is the Lord Almighty;
the whole earth is full of his glory."

At the sound of their voices the doorposts and thresholds shook and the temple was filled with smoke.

"Woe to me!" I cried. "I am ruined! For I am a man of unclean lips, and I live among a people of unclean lips, and my eyes have seen the King, the Lord Almighty."

Then one of the seraphs flew to me with a live coal in his hand, which he had taken with tongs from the altar. With it he touched my mouth and said, "See, this has touched your lips; your guilt is taken away and your sin atoned for."

Then I heard the voice of the Lord saying, "Whom shall I send?And who will go for us?"

And I said, "Here am I. Send me!" (Isa. 6:1-8).

First, Isaiah "saw the Lord . . . high and exalted" (v. 1). The desire of the people of God in every generation was realized in this man. He was granted a glimpse into heaven's throne room. What he saw was more wonderful than could be described and had a profound impact on Isaiah.

Second, he confessed his sinfulness as "a man of unclean lips" (v. 5). So grand was his vision of Yahweh in his splendor that Isaiah was compelled to respond with an explanation of his own status. He claimed no right to what he had seen. To the contrary, he disclaimed any such right and acknowledged his unworthiness.

Third, he received divine purification when an angel touched his lips with a live coal from the altar and said, "Your guilt is taken away and your sin atoned for" (v. 7). As always, salvation is a matter of grace. The soon-to-be prophet was not told of a redemption that would be his at the end of his ministry but was given cleansing as a prerequisite for undertaking it.

Fourth, Isaiah heard and heeded the divine call—that his life be yielded to God for prophetic ministry—when he said, "Here am I. Send me!" (v. 8).

Why is this text offered as a model for worship? True worship must begin with a vision of God rather than with a commitment to self-gratification. Then, acutely conscious of God, each worshiper sees himself and his world more clearly, identifies the distractions in her life that would keep her from God, and submits all things to God for the sake of atonement, purification, and healing. The worship encounter results in a clarified sense of spiritual direction for daily living. Reverence thus proves to be at the very heart of relevance.

While worship is not an escape from ethics, neither is worship the mere servant of ethics. Like art (*Ars gratia ars*), worship is its own reward. To *use* the church's worship for any human purpose other than the glorification of God is to abuse it. . . . However, it is also true that while we worship God, we are also being formed into God's people. While we are attempting to see God, we are acquiring, as a kind of by-product, a vision of who we are and who we are meant to be.[5]

Against the danger of being misunderstood by calling Isaiah 6 a "paradigm for God-directed worship," we do not mean to imply that it is a rigid pattern. Only occasionally do worship settings involve the commissioning of individuals for prophetic tasks. At other times, they will be celebrational or prayerful or penitential in nature. Most often, perhaps, our corporate experiences of worship are initiated out of a life routine that causes us to go to a certain place at a certain time. The "tone" of the service will be established only after participation has begun.

By offering Isaiah 6 as a model for worship, we plead for a recognition of three factors. (1) True worship centers on God rather than the worshipers; its goal is to see him more clearly rather than to arouse certain emotions in us. (2) When God is encountered in worship, there is a sense of judgment against and perspective on life that comes from no other experience; sin is judged, trivial pursuits are seen for

---

5. Willimon, *Service of God,* pp. 42-43.

what they are, and life is viewed from the prospect of eternity. (3) Empowering grace is mediated to each worshiper; redemption is made personal, its acknowledgment is initiated, and its implications for life past the immediate worshipful context begin to dawn.

Because God desires worship (John 4:23), it is an activity of submission on our part. Because of our urgent need for God (Psa. 130), worship satisfies the human need for communion with him. Because of God's constant goodness to us (Jas. 1:17), it offers us the opportunity of conscious thanksgiving to him. Most fundamental of all reasons for worship, however, is the fact that worship is the adoration of God for who he is. It is the appropriate awe, wonder, and reverence for a creature to give his Creator.

Things That Hinder Worship

If all that has been said to this point about worship is true, then why are we frequently disenchanted with the experience? Why do so many complain that something is missing from their attempts at worship? There are probably many factors working against meaningful worship. Among all that might be named, three are notorious in their ability to abort the devotion God deserves.

First is the *creature-centeredness* that has already been cited. The original sin of the human race was to place itself at the center of things and to judge all things against its selfish concerns. This same sin lies at the heart of our failures in worship. It is what moves us to seek entertainment and to judge worship as a performance to be graded. It is what drives us to expect certain emotional sensations or to expect worship to provide a "rosier outlook on life" for those who participate in it.

Second, attempts at worship are diminished by a *worshiper's insensitivity to God* in the routine of life. This point is made repeatedly in the Word of God. Nowhere is it more emphatic than in Isaiah 1:11-17. This text smacks of a prohibition of any future worship. It has Yahweh rebuking the people by asking, "The multitude of your sacrifices—what are they to me?" His own answer comes back in several forms: "I have more than enough . . . I have no pleasure . . . I cannot bear your evil assemblies . . . They have become a burden to me." Yet it is clear that the point of this prophetic word is not to call for a cessation of public worship but to require that it be offered by people whose hearts and behavior were consecrated to the Lord in daily righteousness. Thus the crescendo of the passage exhorts the people to holiness:

> Stop doing wrong,
>   learn to do right!
> Seek justice,
>   encourage the oppressed.
> Defend the cause of the fatherless,
>   plead the case of the widow (vv. 16b-17).

Worship is inseparable from the affairs of daily life. Thus any concept of Christianity which so formalizes worship that it can be isolated from daily personal conduct must be renounced by right-thinking people. As Jesus told a Samaritan woman beside Jacob's well, the critical issues of worship are no longer place, time, and ritual. These were the old disputes between Jews and Samaritans. Now that the kingdom has come in Christ's own person, worship has new priorities. "A time is coming and has now come," said Jesus, "when the true worshipers will worship the Father in spirit and truth" (John 4:23a). To worship "in spirit" is likely not a reference to the Holy Spirit but to a regenerated human spirit; it is to offer the spiritual worship of a contrite, adoring, and renewed heart. To worship "in truth" is to be understood against the Hebrew concept of truth as integrity, faithfulness, and right behavior as opposed to the Greek notion of truth as factual statements; it is to worship with the whole of one's life laid bare before the Lord for scrutiny, cleansing, and redirection.

Third, we impoverish our worship by *restricting it with tradition*. The development of traditions is inevitable and even helpful, but they must not be elevated to the status of law. Otherwise they become stifling, close off creativity arising from the Spirit of God, and reduce the worshiping body of Christ to a rigid formality.

All evangelical churches struggle with our Puritan heritage that makes the sermon the crescendo of worship and subordinates everything else to it. While we would not be guilty of depreciating the ministry of the Word of God that is our calling, it is nonetheless true that worship sometimes suffers from the choking off of other activities for the sake of allowing the preacher to be a star. If the word "star" offends in this context, think of what has happened with televangelism. It has left the impression that the heart of worship is preaching and that the central figure in the event is the preacher. The structure of many of our church assemblies says the same thing. Even the furniture arrangement customarily supports such a conclusion. One who comes as a stranger to a typical Christian assembly might well leave with the impression that the address of one highly important person from a raised pulpit before a hushed group of passive listeners is the essence of worship.

Contemporary as well as traditional music has its place in worship. Individuals, groups, and the entire congregation may offer the music under different circumstances (1 Cor. 14:26). Written prayers as well as extemporaneous ones are appropriate. Silence and hubbub, planned and spontaneous services, children and adults—all have their place. Yet a repressive tradition will likely dictate a narrow range of possibilities and confine worship to a predictable routine. The church must be open to the invigorating presence of the Spirit's fresh breezes through our sometimes stuffy worship experiences.

Public and Private Worship

For people who would know God, there must be deliberate and intense periods of seeking after him in worship. But this statement must not be understood to refer to corporate worship alone. The majority of these "periods of seeking after him in worship" will be in private places.

In our frantic world of the 21st century, private worship cannot occur by accident. It will have to be deliberate, a matter of discipline by the power of the Holy Spirit (cf. Gal. 5:22-23). Call these episodes of private worship "quiet times," "devotionals," or whatever you like. But they are absolutely essential to spiritual life and health. Just as musicians practice hours and hours in private for occasional public performances, so Christians who wish to worship meaningfully in corporate settings must undergird those with hours of private worship. Yet this may be a poor figure to use. It could suggest that private worship is only a form of training for the "real event" of group worship. That is not our point at all. Each experience of worship has its own intrinsic value. The musician metaphor is designed only to illustrate how foolish it would be to expect to worship meaningfully in a corporate worship time if there is no daily experience of private worship. Perhaps the reason so many leave the public place of worship lamenting that they "got nothing out of it" relates directly to the fact that they have no involvement with or appreciation for worship except as strangers who occasionally drop in on others' performance of this wondrous activity.

Private worship centers principally on the Word of God and prayer. It will include such things as seasons of Bible reading and quietness before the Lord, times of meditation, and occasions of fasting and confession. These can—and ought to be—enriching and empowering events of encounter with God. Not every day will have the powerful impact of every other, but each nourishes the soul and grounds it deeper in a sense of wonder and awe before the Almighty.

Calling these "private" times of worship is not to say that some of them will not be shared. Family devotional times are certainly worship experiences. There may also be events of confession and prayer with a spiritual confidant. Or a small group of people may meet periodically to pursue nearness to God through fellowship, study, and prayer.

Corporate worship is presupposed in Scripture. In the most ancient of times, patriarchs led their families in worship and were responsible for sacrifice. When Moses received the covenant at Sinai, worship was changed for the Hebrew nation. A pattern for the tabernacle was given to Moses, and Solomon later beautified and made a more permanent structure for the nation according to the same basic plan. Whether in the desert or in their promised land, that God's people should worship him collectively was taken for granted. When circumstances forced the Jews into a different situation and made the temple inaccessible, the synagogue emerged and there evolved a simple worship involving the reading of Scripture, prayers, the singing of hymns, and a sermon. The absence of sacrifice made synagogue worship quite different from what had taken place at the temple.

Jesus was reared in an environment where the synagogue was central to life. He worshiped there, as did his earliest followers. So strong was the tie between the synagogue and Christianity that what we call "the early church" was often taken to be a

Jewish sect.[6] Because of its strong link to the synagogue, early Christian worship adopted its tradition of reading the Scripture, prayers, the singing
of hymns, and the sermon as its own order of service. To these was added the Lord's Supper.

What we typically think of as public worship is
the full church in assembly. Corporate worship of
this sort is a form of collective wonder and awe before God that is expressed in culturally relevant
ways. The tone of these large-group worship experiences will vary. Some will be events of praise and
celebration honoring God as God. Others will emphasize teaching and exhortation. Still others will
be times of tearful sharing and penitence. When
the Spirit of God is present, it will not always be
possible to determine the atmosphere in advance.
Leaders may intend and prepare for a service of
one sort, and God may bring about another end to
his glory.

While the practical details of implementing a
theology of worship must be left to individual fellowships and congregations, we dare to offer a few
suggestions about areas crying out for creative and
Spirit-guided attention.

Hymnody. We strongly urge the development of
a contemporary hymnody to supplement the redis-

---

6. The Roman proconsul before whom Paul appeared in Corinth
(i.e., Gallio, A.D. 51-52, cf. Acts 18:12ff) seems clearly to have regarded the two groups as part of the same religion. So long as the
two were seen this way, Christianity enjoyed legal status within the
Roman system. Sometime between A.D. 50 and the great fire in
Rome of July A.D. 64, the two came to be distinguished. In connection with the latter event, Christianity was challenged by the government while Judaism maintained its status as a legal religion.

covery of the best of the church's accustomed music. What does it say about the spiritual acumen of a religious tradition that has ceased to produce songs of praise and prayer worthy of our use? Urban churches continue to sing hymns built on agricultural and nautical metaphors when neither is our context any longer. In examining one widely used book of church songs, we were able to find only one out of 600 that had a clearly urban setting. Praise ought to be in relevant words and images, and it needs to be set to contemporary music.

We urge that hymns with a vertical orientation be given predominance over songs with a horizontal orientation. That is, let there be more hymns of praise and prayer addressed directly to God (e.g., "To God Be the Glory," "Bless His Holy Name," "There's Something About That Name," *et al.*) and fewer designed to encourage believers to do one thing or another (e.g., "Rise Up, O Church of God," "For You I Am Praying," "Onward, Christian Soldiers," *et al.*). The hymnody of a Christ-focused church should serve primarily to direct our eyes above, not fix our gaze on one another. Whether sung by the entire body or presented by one person or a small group to the larger group, our songs should lift our view above ourselves to God.

We also suggest something of a simplification of church music. Music has the marvelous power to focus a group's confession of faith in a way that mere recitation never could. But far too often the complicated, ornate, or "jazzy" style of the music appeals to the ear without quickening the spiritual man. If one were merely to read much of what we sing, freed from the trappings of its flashy music, it would be evident that the words hardly bear saying once—much less constant repetition.

Public Prayer. We suggest the writing and reading of more public prayers. Extemporaneous prayers are proper and will remain the norm in most evangelical settings. Yet this process can be trivialized by thoughtlessness, routine, and rote. Michel Quoist's enduring classic *Prayers of Life* shows the power of thoughtfully worded, spiritually sensitive, written prayers to speak the hearts and minds of all.

Leading the hearts and minds of whole congregations to the throne of God is a serious responsibility which deserves much thought and prayer. While spontaneous prayer is often appropriate, it is a companion to written prayer rather than a substitute for it. Think what a blessing would come to our worship if we produced people who wrote modern psalms to voice our deepest needs and concerns.

The Word. We encourage the development of more theological preaching. The foremost point of preaching in worship is to give the worshipers a clearer vision of God. This task is both primary to and foundational for ethical instruction or motivational preaching. Preaching should inspire worship by lifting up God. It should be neither discontinuous with nor dominant over the assembly; it should rather serve to help focus the worshiper's eyes on the object of our faith and love.

There also needs to be a recommitment to the public reading of Scripture, especially the Psalms.

Too often the only biblical text read in an assembly are the few verses that serve as the text for the preacher's sermon. The Word of God deserves a stronger voice in our midst. A reemphasis on our respect for the Bible as God's Word to us will be enhanced as we hear it read intelligibly in our assemblies.

With some reservation, we also suggest the use of testimony in the assembly. By the term, we mean the public proclamation of the presence of God in an individual's own life. While this is no *substitute* for the preaching of the biblical text, there needs to be room in our assemblies for people to share the *personal* faith that fuels our very existence as the people of God. Preachers routinely speak of their personal faith and spiritual experiences. Who is to say that others in the congregation do not have stories to tell that are of equal or greater value?

Structure. We offer three suggestions in the area of structure and programming of public worship.

First, variety in the order of presentation is strongly recommended. Many of our worship assemblies are so predictable that the tendency is to put ourselves on auto-pilot and perform on cue. Variety helps keep us alert in our participation. Comfort with a certain way of doing things is too often complacency or, worse yet, a type of idolatry in which we confuse the form with the reality. Of course it is possible for our zeal for variety to cause us to focus on how things are done rather than on the object of our worship, so care must be taken here. Still, the fact remains that our more accus-

tomed problem has been stagnation, not overzeal-
ous variety.

Second, we need to strive for an atmosphere that
respects the sensibilities of a wide spectrum of worshipers. There is a place in worship for raucous celebration; there is a place for awestruck contemplation. There is a place for spontaneity; there is a
place for carefully planned liturgy. There is a place
for silence; there is a place for speaking. None of us
has the right to dictate how things always must be.
We have no right to quench the infinite variety of
loving responses to the presence of God. Mutual respect and concern will lead us into unselfish acceptance and praise to God for our brothers' and sisters'
offering of praise, even when it is in ways to which
we are not personally disposed.

Third, we plead for the Lord's Supper to be the
focal point of the church's corporate worship. The
justification for this plea stems from its unique call
to the body and blood of Jesus. So important is the
Lord's Supper to the total experience of the church
that it is deferred for discussion until Chapter Ten.

Conclusion

That we could so spoil worship as to make it
dull and boring to ourselves and unattractive to
non-Christians is scandalous. We must recapture
the spirit of worship and refuse to let it be mere
routine.

As with Isaiah's experience of old, true worship
must begin with a vision of God. High and lifted up
before us, all else both fades in its own significance
and is placed in its proper relationship to eternity.

Confronted by this God, we will feel and confess our unworthiness before him. Yet reminded again of the cross, we will feel the exhilaration of pardon and offer ourselves as willing servants to God in the world. There will be jubilation on occasion— perhaps with applause and cheering. At other times, there may be pensive melancholy or abundant tears. There will be experiences others will attempt to duplicate by manipulating emotions and repeating procedures, but the second-level imitations will be shoddy. They will have originated with man and will be designed to satisfy man. True worship always proceeds from a God-directed goal and can arise from no other orientation of the heart.

May God help us to rise above the familiar, comfortable, and routine to worship him in spirit and in truth.

CHAPTER SEVEN

Life:
The Church Relates to Itself

No matter how beautiful a neighborhood may be from the outside, someone considering moving in wants to know what kind of life really goes on there. The same is true of the church. No matter how beautiful the building or "exciting" the worship time, one who intends to live within the group still wants to know that authentic spiritual life is present. There are certain dynamics that must be unmistakable in the internal workings of the body if we are to make a serious claim to the continuing presence of Christ in our midst. In this chapter we want to examine the three most basic components of church life—compassion, encouragement, and confession.

Compassion

"This is how we know what love is: Jesus Christ laid down his life for us. And we ought to lay down our lives for our brothers. If anyone has material possessions and sees his brother in need but has no pity on him, how can the love of God be in him? Dear children, let us not love with words or tongue but with actions and in truth" (1 John 3:16-18). To this New Testament exhortation, hurting people cry, "Amen! Amen!"

From the very beginning, the church has been marked by compassionate concern for each of its members. This compassion is not mere sentimentality but active involvement on behalf of one another's welfare. It is one of the primary indicators of the presence of the living Lord within his spiritual body.

The point we wish to stress just here is that compassion in the church is always marked by concrete, directed activity. Many of us are familiar with the Kierkegaardian concept of *angst* or the term "free-floating anxiety." This is different from concrete fear where we know what is making us afraid. When the bear is chasing us, our fear has a very definite object. But when we experience "free-floating anxiety," we cannot be specific about the object of our fear. It is not directed at any particular object.

Compassion in the church is never free-floating. It is not some sort of general goodwill that is never directed at anyone in particular. It always expresses itself in concrete acts on behalf of an identifiable someone. "Suppose a brother or sister is without clothes and daily food. If one of you says to him, 'Go, I wish you well; keep warm and well fed,' but does nothing about his physical needs, what good is it?" (Jas. 2:15-16).

There is a real sense in which the church becomes a kind of School of Compassion. It is where we learn _how_ to love. By learning to respond to the needs of the community of faith, we learn how to transform the love of Christ into meaningful assistance.

There was a young woman in a church we know. She was a new convert who was inexperienced with and terrified by people with handicaps. In this church, however, there were several blind members. Filled with the love of Christ, she was convinced she ought to reach out in fellowship and service to these sisters and brothers. Starting from a place where she was afraid even to touch them, she began doing simple tasks for them such as guiding them around the building. Before too long, she was taking some of them shopping. Eventually she found herself ministering to them in ways she would never have dreamed possible. The fear disappeared and was replaced by genuine Christian compassion. What she discovered along the way was not only helpful to others but personally liberating.

Joseph Fletcher made the term "situation ethics" popular in the 1960s. He proposed that one should "love and do what you will." He was convinced there was no set of rules that could tell one what to do in each unique situation. But, of course, the great problem with Fletcher's proposal is that it gives no guidance in knowing what the loving thing to do really is.

It is in this area of learning _how_ to care about people that the church plays a crucial role. As with the young woman mentioned above, there is an at-

mosphere of concern and openness in the church.
There is a deep commitment to *be Jesus* in the
faithful church that leads us into the life of active
compassion.

When we read the apostle Paul appreciatively,
he leads us into the discovery of a relational ethic.
How do we know how to act? We first consider
what is in the best interest of our brother. The test
case Paul employs is the question of whether a
Christian may eat meat that has been involved in
idol worship. Paul contends that, while there is
nothing inherently wrong with eating such meat,
our major consideration must be how our participation will influence our fellow believers. If there is
good reason to think the action will lead to the
detriment of a fellow believer, love will lead us to
forego what we otherwise would be free to do.

Paul's position may initially strike us as absurd.
Why should my freedom be curbed by someone
else's foundationless hang-ups? But Paul is concerned with the more fundamental principle of
compassion. It is his way of translating the theological notion of the imitation of Christ into concrete action. Just as Jesus gave up the privilege of
heaven for our sakes, so must we be willing to give
up some of our desires and deeds for the sake of
brothers and sisters given to us by the Lord.

The point that Jesus' disciples are identified primarily by their love for each other has been made so
often that it has almost become trite, so perhaps our
readers need no convincing on the point. We only
hope to suggest that practicing true, consistent,
Christlike compassion is a task that takes a lifetime

of nurturing in a compassionate community. The practice of compassion is never easy.

So the church becomes a place where we teach each other how to care for people. We learn to treat the handicapped as the real people they are; we learn to give to the poor without condescension or patronage; we learn to be with the grieving though we feel uncomfortable and don't know what to say; we learn to pray with the sick though hospitals make us nervous; we learn to celebrate with the successes of our fellows though we once considered everyone's success but our own a threat; we learn to accept the help of others graciously in spite of the fact that we have been taught to be "independent"; and, most important of all, we learn not to insist on our own way all the time but to consider the welfare of the other.

Many of us do not realize how much we learn about caring for people in a good congregation, but it is central to who we are as the body of Christ. Every Christian occasionally ought to ask: What do my fellow Christians learn about compassion *from me*?

Encouragement

Christians will always find themselves aliens in a hostile world. "Do not be surprised, my brothers, if the world hates you" (1 John 3:13). When a single solitary Christian lines up against the world, it is often a woeful mismatch. That is why it is so crucial that the Christian never find himself without the support and encouragement of other Christians in the church. A famous passage in Hebrews emphasizes the need for mutual encouragement, especially in the context of impending crisis. "And let us consider how we may spur one another on toward love and good deeds. Let us not give up meeting together, as some are in the habit of doing, but let us encourage one another—and all the more as you see the Day approaching" (Heb. 10:24-25).

We may harbor romantic notions about the brave Christian standing absolutely alone against all the Devil's onslaughts. But the plain fact is that for most of us this is the most terrifying of all prospects. All of us know stories of some courageous soul who stood against the world and all its fury—only to collapse like a house of cards when abandoned by family or friends.

Of course, personal responsibility is important. The individual believer must take her stand for righteousness. A Christian man must be willing to face temptation with determination. Our point is to emphasize the group as the context in which personal responsibility is accepted and lived.

> All this is not to suggest that there is anything unreal about individual responsibility. But this is always responsibility *to someone else* and it is always learned *with someone else*. An individual whose moral experiences never reached beyond "monologue" would know nothing at all about responsibility.[1]

We experience the moral life as a series of responsibilities to different groups of which we are

---

1. Michael Walzer, *Obligations* (Cambridge: Harvard University Press, 1970), p. 22.

members. Some of these are very distant groups, and others are more intimate. We are not members of these groups in serial order but simultaneously. For instance, we have obligations to the nation as citizens of the United States, obligations to our employers as members of the firm, obligations to our families (the most intimate group), obligations to the churches of which we are members, and obligations to other associations that could be listed. Each of these groups has a value system in which it expects us to invest ourselves and participate. But what happens when the value systems of these various groups conflict? What do we do then?

The first experience of this sort of conflict for most of us probably took place between family values and the peer group—much to our parents' chagrin. Children are often torn between loyalty to their classmates and obligation to school authorities. And competing loyalties continue to be a mark of the adult moral life. One may be torn between obligations to a narrower racial/ethnic heritage and broader national policy; the conflict may be between the values of church and business.

It is, of course, the conflict between the values of God as advanced by a kingdom-seeking church and other value systems that predominantly concerns us here. One could point to obvious conflicts like those between believers from pacifist traditions and the government in war times, but we wish to emphasize the more subtle everyday contest between worldliness and Christianity. The church is inextricably involved in this conflict.

The dynamic we are discussing is encouragement. Encouragement is the total process by means of which the church supports individual Christians in the maintaining of biblical values and lifestyles against all competitors. Too many Christians succumb to worldliness because they have no strong home base from which to work. It is fundamental to the life of the church that individual Christians find encouragement to stand against the demands of other groups with which they are also associated.

It is a truism that in the business world there is incredible pressure to cut corners to get or stay ahead. How are the millions of Christians who are involved in corporations, from the bottom all the way up to positions of extreme power, going to cope with this pressure? The church is not performing properly if it does not provide the support to withstand such temptation. And support of this sort cannot be given just by preaching the platitudes of honesty; it must come through providing forums for encouragement of one another in word and prayer. Christians will frequently find themselves in a conflict between the values of Christ and the demands of their companies for success. Apart from a dynamic group that produces a counterbalance, the company will often overpower the individual. That is why the church must be about the ministry of encouragement.

This has long been seen to be true in the case of teenagers. This is why many congregations have built youth programs headed up by professional youth ministers. It is an attempt to create a peer group to counter another peer group that is attempting to instill values of which Christian parents do not approve. It is really quite remarkable that we have not seen that this same dynamic is essential at all levels of Christian maturity.

Only by constant reinforcement in a caring community will Christian values survive in an alien world. The world lives for today, but Christians look to eternity; the world emphasizes pleasure, while Christians stress character; the world teaches the relativity of all values, while Christians commit themselves to the abiding Word of God. And so it goes.

We offer only a couple of suggestions on how the ministry of encouragement can be enhanced. Encouragement is something that cannot be "programmed" in a systematic way. We will have to be sensitive and creative to find appropriate means of carrying out this critical ministry.

First, the church must use the concept of peer groups. There are many issues that are best handled by persons other than professional ministers. Open, pointed, Bible-centered discussion about value conflicts by people on the firing line may accomplish more than a dozen sermons on the given topic. Medical professionals, business leaders, educators, entertainers and artists, working mothers, parents with school-age children, teenagers, and many others share unique challenges that provide rich experience for Christian reflection. We must facilitate their opportunities and abilities to minister to one another.

Second, the church must nurture moral development. Christians do not need simple solutions to complex dilemmas. What they do need is an opportunity to think through these problems in the context of faith. The church's job is to provide this opportunity for biblically informed, Christ-centered discussion of life's challenges.

We are suggesting that teaching correct rules of behavior will not necessarily create Christian virtue. We further contend that merely following the accepted norms of the group is inadequate to deal with the moral demands of the workplace. The church seeks to provide a total atmosphere in which the will of God expressed in law becomes the authentic mindset of the believers nurtured in it. Thus the Christian is empowered to respond to situations not specifically addressed by Scripture by virtue of a transformed character.

We live in a world where many groups have their claws in us. If we are to be truly Christlike in this world, we will need each other's constant encouragement. From the outset, Jesus had 12 disciples—not one. As support groups such as Alcoholics Anonymous are discovering and implementing the dynamic of peer groups formed around common concerns and goals, they are implementing Jesus' teaching and example. It would be a shame for the church to omit something so vital from its life.

Confession

The third element of the life of the church that must be considered in this chapter is *confession*. In some ways it is the most crucial, for it is often the focal point where compassion and encouragement find concrete expression. It is also the point at which doctrine and life meet, for it is the real-life expression of the doctrine of the pilgrim church and divine grace.

Confession is crucial to the life of the church because to be a Christian does not mean to be sinless. As John points out to his Christian readers: "If we claim to be without sin, we deceive ourselves and the truth is not in us. . . . If we claim we have not sinned, we make him out to be a liar and his word has no place in our lives" (1 John 1:8,10). Given this truth, how Christians handle their sin is crucial to the effective living of discipleship.

There are three broadly different ways that Christians deal with our continuing sinfulness. First, we can take sin lightly. That is, we sin and then simply go on our merry way. We feel no guilt for our sin, and in fact, we come to the point where we hardly even notice it.

The problems with such an approach should be obvious. How can we fail to take seriously that for which Jesus died? "While we were still sinners, Christ died for us." (Rom. 5:8). Sin separates us from God. It hurts the one we love. It demands to be taken seriously.

The second way of dealing with sin is to become such a guilt-ridden neurotic that one is eventually paralyzed by guilt and fear and self-condemnation. This person takes sin seriously but, unfortunately, is unable to believe in God's forgiveness. So this Christian is constantly worried about whether he or she is really saved. The joy of Christianity is drowned in a self-imposed condemnation in which the conviction is not "once saved, always saved" but "if saved, barely saved." What a nightmarish existence.

The third way of dealing with sin is God's way. Here sin is taken with the deadly seriousness of the cross. Yet the wonderful truth of God's gracious forgiveness is taken with equal seriousness. As we confess our sins to God, we believe that he freely and totally forgives us. Thus we live with neither a careless attitude toward sin nor guilt-ridden neurosis.

In Psalm 32, David verbalizes something of the power of unconfessed sin in our lives—and the greater power of confession.

> Blessed is he
>> whose transgressions are forgiven,
>> whose sins are covered.
> Blessed is the man
>> whose sin the Lord does not count
>>> against him
>> and in whose spirit is no deceit.
> When I kept silent,
>> my bones wasted away
>> through my groaning all day long.
> For day and night
>> your hand was heavy upon me;
> my strength was sapped
>> as in the heat of summer.
> Then I acknowledged my sin to you
>> and did not cover up my iniquity.
> I said, "I will confess
>> my transgressions to the Lord"—
> and you forgave
>> the guilt of my sin (Psa. 32:1-5).

Here David revels in his discovery that the only relief from the oppressiveness of sin is to confess the
sin to God and to experience his forgiveness in the
process.

The most important passage in the New
Testament on this matter of confession is from the
pen of the apostle John:

> This is the message we have heard from
> him and declare to you: God is light; in him
> there is no darkness at all. If we claim to have
> fellowship with him yet walk in the darkness,
> we lie and do not live by the truth. But if we
> walk in the light, as he is in the light, we have
> fellowship with one another, and the blood of
> Jesus, his Son, purifies us from all sin.
>
> If we claim to be without sin, we deceive
> ourselves and the truth is not in us. If we con-
> fess our sins, he is faithful and just and will
> forgive us our sins and purify us from all un-
> righteousness. If we claim we have not
> sinned, we make him out to be a liar and his
> word has no place in our lives (1 John 1:5-10).

John points out that even though a Christian
still commits sins, the blood of Jesus cleanses the
believer as he walks in the light. To "walk in the
light," at least in part, means to confess one's sins
to God. Now one must be careful here not to make
John say just the opposite of what he intends. He is
trying to reassure Christians of their forgiveness.

John unquestionably does not mean that if
someone confesses at 10:00, sins at 11:00, and dies
at 12:00, that wretched soul will be in hell by 1:00!

He is depicting two broadly different lifestyles. For the person who shakes a fist at God and insists "You can't tell me what to do!" there can be no forgiveness. But for the person who is trying to serve God and is sorry when he or she hurts God, the assurance of God's forgiveness is constant. We might call this "confessional living." So there is no need to keep a "sin journal" as some have done to make sure no sin goes unconfessed lest one be condemned.

But all of this is between God and a particular individual. So what does it have to do with the church? In James 5:16, other Christians are brought into the picture: "Therefore confess your sins to each other and pray for each other so that you may be healed. The prayer of a righteous man is powerful and effective."

But why confess to another Christian? Won't God forgive me without someone else knowing? Of course he will. But perhaps that misses the point.

> Who can give us certainty that, in the confession and the forgiveness of our sins, we are not dealing with ourselves but with the living God? God gives us this certainty through our brother. Our brother breaks the circle of self-deception. A man who confesses his sins in the presence of a brother knows that he is no longer alone with himself; he experiences the presence of God in the reality of the other person. As long as I am by myself in the confession of my sins everything remains in the dark, but in the presence of a brother the sin has to be brought into the light. But since the

sin must come to light sometime, it is better
that it happens today between me and my
brother, rather than on the last day in the
piercing light of the final judgment. It is a
mercy that we can confess our sins to a
brother. Such grace spares us the terrors of
the last judgment.

Our brother has been given me that even
here and now I may be made certain through
him of the reality of God in His judgment and
His grace. As the open confession of my sins
to a brother insures me against self-deception,
so, too, the assurance of forgiveness becomes
fully certain to me only when it is spoken by a
brother in the name of God. Mutual, brotherly
confession is given to us by God in order that
we may be sure of divine forgiveness.[2]

As Bonhoeffer points out, there are several ben-
efits that come from sharing a confession of sin
with another. Let us highlight only three here.
First, we receive *assurance*. Many of us find it hard
to believe that God really forgives us, but in the re-
assurance of our brother, we experience that forgiveness in a tangible way. The forgiving Christ
comes to us enfleshed again through some member
of his spiritual body to bring the conviction of acceptance by those who know of the sin only to respond with grace.

Second, we are protected from *self-deception*. It
is difficult to be glib and frivolous when laying our
sin before another. If we are inclined to evade tak-

2. Dietrich Bonhoeffer, *Life Together*, translated by John W.
Doberstein (New York: Harper & Row, 1954), pp. 116-117.

ing our sin seriously, confession to a brother may help us give due weight to our sin.

Third, confession greatly *decreases the power of the sin*. Sin loves the darkness. Think about how much energy and effort we employ to keep from being found out. When sin is brought to light, much of its power is lost. Wrestling lone with sin in the darkness often requires that more sins (e.g., evasions, lies, etc.) be committed in an effort to cover the former one. Think of David's horrible downward spiral in his attempts to mask his sin with Bathsheba.

There was a time in the history of God's people when only certain designated individuals could serve to mediate between the people and God. These men were the priests. But now every Christian is a priest. This truth has a dual application. First, you can go directly to God on your own behalf; you can be your own priest. Second, you also can go to any other Christian to intercede to God for you; any other Christian can function as a priest for you.

One of the church's most important and unique ministries is allowing each of its members to function as a "priest" for any other member. But the sad fact is that many of us are horribly uncomfortable in the role of either confessor or priest. So, lest we neglect and fail in this critical calling, we close this section with a few practical suggestions on the giving and receiving of confession.

In the giving of confession, the first consideration is choosing a priest. We do not encourage Christians to run around telling everyone all the wrong things he or she has done—or thought about doing. This is simply irresponsible. One should instead select a spiritually mature Christian who will be able to handle whatever is said with grace and seriousness. Trust is an absolute necessity in the confessor-priest relationship, so we suggest choosing someone who has already displayed a genuine concern for your spiritual welfare.

A second essential in sharing a confession is that we be both specific and penetrating in the confession. Richard Foster writes: "A generalized confession may save us from humiliation and shame but it will not ignite inward healing."[3] But we must not fall into the trap of confessing a list of sins without simultaneously searching our hearts for the roots out of which these branches grow. It is much easier to admit a mistake committed out of weakness than to admit a fundamental flaw in our Christian character that nourishes these improprieties. So there is a need to be specific about sins of act and attitude.

There is also the need to cultivate repentance in our confession. When we confess our sin, it ought to be with the attitude that it will never, never happen again. Those of us who have lived very long know this will not always be the case, but sin should bring us such pain in what it does to us, God, and others that we determine henceforth to avoid it at all costs.

Then we must accept forgiveness and move on. As Tillich puts it, we must have the courage to "ac-

---

3. Richard J. Foster, *Celebration of Discipline* (New York: Harper & Row, Publishers, 1978), p. 132.

cept ourselves as accepted even though we are unacceptable."[4] Perhaps the greatest gift of grace is
the courage to live life imperfectly, for we can live it
no other way.

On this point, we also feel compelled to offer a
few suggestions for those times when we are called
to receive the confession of a brother or sister. The
first rule is very simple: listen. The second rule is
similar but more emphatic: *listen.* And the third
rule is the most important of all: *listen!*

This part of the priestly role cannot be stressed
too much. There is an incredible urge, when someone is conveying something painful, to break in and
make it better. Though understandable, this is a
temptation to be resisted with determination. This
kind of interference often short-circuits the process
of the confessor's attempt to unburden a breaking
heart. We have experienced occasions when it took
the person several hours—and several side-trips—
to finally confess the sin that was eating away at
spiritual life and peace. Sin seldom comes to the
light without being dragged out, fighting all the
way, and your role as priest is patient listening. If
it seems necessary, you may need to prod gently
(e.g., "I sense there is something you want to tell
me but haven't been able to bring yourself to say"),
but patience is most often the key.

A priest must also take the sin being confessed
as seriously as the confessor does. Again, the great
temptation will be to say something to make the
person feel better. "Everyone has this problem" or

---

4. Paul Tillich, *The Courage to Be* (New Haven: Yale University
Press, 1952), p. 164.

"That's not really so bad" is a poor and counter-productive response. You must understand that the person will not be able to take your pronouncement of forgiveness seriously if he or she does not believe you have taken the sin seriously. We commonly respond to a confession by saying, "I've heard what you have told me, and you are right to confess it. It is a sin."

Of course there must always be a prayer of forgiveness. This important prayer must not only ask God for forgiveness but also should be a prayer of gratitude for the forgiveness he has bestowed. Along with earnest petition, there must be a faith-claim on divine pardon.

Frequently a sensitive priest will affirm not only that God has forgiven the confessor, but that he or she has as well. If the confessor can look in your eyes and truly believe you have heard the confession and unquestionably forgiven him, he may well believe God has forgiven him, too.

It goes without saying that complete confidentiality is the rule in receiving confession and that the confessional relationship is to be freely chosen but never compelled. Confession is not a manipulative club to keep people in line; it is a blessing from God.

And it also should be noted that ministers, elders, and other church leaders are particularly in need of this confessing relationship. They are so often the receivers of confession that they may overlook their own need for a priest. Church leaders are so much in the public eye that they must often be towers of strength whether they feel that

way or not. It is not easy for church leaders to confess their own sins and inadequacies, for their congregations will not often want to hear such a revelation. It is all the more crucial that they find some
mature, spiritually sensitive Christian with whom
to share their burdens and sins. There is no easier
target for Satan than a minister who has started to
believe his own press.

Can we catch a vision of the confessing church?
A church of saved sinners rather than perfect
saints? A church where sin is never belittled and
yet never allowed to fester and destroy in the darkness? A church where the norm is transparency
rather than duplicity? A church where God's forgiveness is experienced as a concrete reality in the
absolution of a brother or sister? A church where
the confessor of sin is not ostracized but embraced?

Sin is, lamentably, a permanent part of our picture. How we deal with our own imperfection will
make all the difference. Can you catch the vision of
the confessing church? God has willed that we be
just such a body of people.

Conclusion

Here, then, is a glimpse into the life of the
church. It is a School of Compassion where its
members learn to put away their own desires and
learn to respond to one another in ways that are
helpful in the real world of everyday life. It is a
place where Christian values are nurtured and en-
couraged in the face of worldly opposition. It is a
confessing community, where sin need be neither
ignored nor hidden but is disarmed and defeated
by openness and forgiveness.

There can be no "doctrinally sound" church where such dynamics are not exhibited. "Soundness" in the Pauline vocabulary refers to a situation of spiritual healthiness, and these are the marks of spiritual health. Regardless of how beautiful a neighborhood is from the outside, we finally want to know what kind of life goes on there. Any vision of the church worth pursuing must carry forward the promise of its Head: "I have come that you might have life and have it to the full" (John 10:10b).

CHAPTER EIGHT

Mission: The Church Relates to the World

Jesus lived his life *in the world*. He was neither mystic nor monk. He demonstrated the life of sonship to the Father during an embodied human existence. If the church is to model its head, it must do the same. All this is to say that there is a real sense in which the church must be *this-worldly*.

From the very beginning of Scripture, it is acknowledged that the world is the legitimate sphere of human activity. In Genesis 1, God authorizes human beings to exercise dominion over the earth. Human cultural and scientific achievements can be seen as a logical extension of this imperative. Human accomplishment is in itself no threat to the prerogatives of deity, and Christians should gladly embrace every effort that can contribute to a more humane world, whether it be artistic, scientific, or political.

Neither should we overlook the fact that Romans 8 pictures redemption as a process so thorough that it includes creation itself. Christians should not be engaged in the wholesale condemnation of the world but rather should be agents for its redemption and transformation. Jesus must have had something like this in mind in the Sermon on the Mount when he used salt as an image of what Christian ministry seeks to achieve. We are not to write off the created order as hopelessly opposed to God—he did create it, remember—but to make ourselves available to God to transform it into the image of Christ.

Nevertheless, the church must not be swallowed up by worldliness. To say that the church must be "this-worldly" is not to defend its involvement with worldly evils or its distraction by worldly pleasures. While Jesus lived his life in the world, his life was thoroughly distinct from it. It is this balance between *transforming engagement with the world* and yet a *spiritual distinction from it* that the church must seek to achieve.

We could define the mission of the church as "living transcendently in the midst of everyday life." The church must never forget that it is a new creation, not dependent on flesh and blood. Nor must it allow itself to become so wrapped up in the contemplation of heaven that it forgets that Earth is the arena of God's glory. Transcendence is not modeled by disconnecting from one's culture. Instead, our attempt is to enliven every cultural task with an awareness of the presence of God, though he cannot be reduced to and fully captured by any cultural or religious manifestations. Our theologies and deeds are never complete as expressions of the divine will. At best, they are hazy images of heavenly things that we execute in the limited medium of human possibilities.

At this point, the question of how all this theological talk is worked out concretely must be addressed. We submit that there are three aspects to the church's mission of modeling transcendence, even in the mundane.

Demonstration

The first aspect of the church's relationship to the world is loving, nurturing service with no strings attached. As Jesus died for us when we had nothing to offer, so we must develop this same mindset. As Philippians 2 says, we must have the self-emptying attitude of Jesus. We must learn not to grasp but to give. Our first move toward every human creature, because he or she was created by God and in his own image, is to love and nurture. It matters not whether we approve or disapprove of the person or his lifestyle. We don't have to worry about judging his actions. We simply love and nurture and serve him as Jesus modeled for us.

This brings a radical transcendence to all of life's activities because we respond to every person we meet not based on human calculation of their worthiness but out of the divine love that does not keep score. We might call this first aspect of our mission *demonstration*.

The church must demonstrate that there is a way to deal with people that is more than human.

Galatians 6:10 states that doing good to all is primary to the church's work and that this "work of mercy" begins with the community of faith. (If we cannot treat each other this way, how can we hope to treat the world with loving service?) Our mission begins with simple, everyday care for people—whatever their needs—because Jesus showed us this is how we are to live.

The call to follow Jesus' example of self-emptying service is the justification for every kind of help program that churches wish to pursue. Counseling, day care, literacy, food and housing, drug and alcohol treatment programs—all are ways of caring for and nurturing people. The church is freed to do these things by the divine love that doesn't keep score. Some are concerned that the church will become just another human do-good agency. But the church *must* be a do-good agency; yet it will never be merely *human* as long as it sees all of its activities as an expression of the redemptive love of God that transcends all human goodness.

A couple of Jesus' more famous teachings help show the transcendent aspect of the church's compassion. In Luke 10, Jesus tells the Good Samaritan story in response to the question "Who is my neighbor?" The point of the story is to show that anyone who is in need is my neighbor. With this story, Jesus creates a whole world of neighbors. As human beings we try to convince ourselves that no one can accept such an extensive responsibility. In his book of poetic meditations entitled *Prayers of Life*, Michel Quoist wrestles with this awesome task, by asking, "Lord, why did you tell

me to love?" He realizes if you open the doors of
your heart to all, there is no end to the world's
needs and one's own comfortable life is threatened.

> Lord, they hurt me! They are in the way, they
> are everywhere.
> They are too hungry; they are consuming me!
>> I can't do anything any more; as they come
>> in, they push the door, and the door opens
>> wider . . .
> Lord! My door is wide open!
>> I can't stand it any more! It's too much! It's
>> no kind of a life!
> What about my job?
>> my family?
>> my peace?
>> my liberty?
>> and me?
> Lord! I have lost everything, I don't belong to
> myself any longer;
> There's no room for me at home.[1]

No merely human love can sustain such ministry; it can only be sustained by transcendent convictions. As Quoist says at his prayer's conclusion:

> Don't worry, God says, you have gained all,
> While men came in to you,
> I, your Father,
> I, your God,
> Slipped in among them.[2]

---

1. Michel Quoist, *Prayers of Life* (Dublin: Gill and Macmillan Ltd.,
1963) p. 91-92.

2. Quoist, *Prayers of Life*, p. 92.

But it is not just the extent of selfless service that requires a more than human response. It is also the nature of the people we are called to serve.

It is sad to have to confess that the church has sometimes been slow to learn that compassionate service is not limited by racial, ethnic, or national lines. This is also clearly part of the teaching of Jesus' Parable of the Good Samaritan. But that lesson is *easy* to learn compared to another principle Jesus insists on in our relationships with the world.

Consider Jesus' answer to another question. How often should I forgive a person? Seven times? Of course you recall Jesus answers "seventy times seven." Have you ever thought about what is being taught here? After all, to forgive a person seven times seems rather generous by human standards. But 490?[3] Obviously, we must begin to question the motives of someone who must be forgiven so constantly. But his motives are immaterial. The question is not whether he *deserves* forgiveness. We simply forgive because God has forgiven us. Our response must not be based on the worthiness of the other but on the heart of God. This is truly transcendent compassion grounded in the heart of God.

This type of behavior cannot be "faked." If we do not care for people in this way, they will see through us. Compassion grounded in purely worldly foundations will not sustain a lifetime of selfless ministry. Only the love of God can so compel us.

---

3. We are aware of the translation problem encountered at Matthew 18:22. Whether correctly translated as "seventy times seven" (KJV) or "seventy-seven times" (NIV), the point is that forgiveness must be without legalistic conditions or limits.

Holiness and Justice

The second part of the church's mission is to call the world to holiness and justice under the reign of God. Evangelism is a crucial part of this task, but it is so important that we will leave it to be discussed in a later lesson. At this point we simply want to emphasize that the church should be an agent to bring about a better world, a world more congenial to all of God's creatures. To serve people genuinely, we not only engage in selfless care for them but must also call them—along with all of their institutions—to holiness.

Leviticus 19 communicates the important truth that holiness is a way of life. It involves care for the poor and strangers, honesty, consideration of the handicapped, and justice in all of the institutions of society. It is part of our mission to call every society, nation, and culture to live under the values of God. We need not turn the church into a political action committee in order for it to be an instrument of God's righteousness.

If the church is to be the cutting edge of the kingdom of God, it must call the world to kingdom living. Injustice, unfairness, greed, selfishness, abuse of power, and dehumanizing activities are all enemies of God and thus enemies of the church. We must not abandon the world to live in our sheltered little forts, but we must take the battle for righteousness to a morally and spiritually impoverished world.

Liberation theologians have continually pointed to a great temptation that faces the church. They warn of the church itself becoming an instrument of the powerful in its society to oppress the poor and disenfranchised. The church then becomes the defender of the respectable status quo and may confuse the radical claims of discipleship with "the good life" of the American success gospel. But, as Gustavo Gutierrez points out, a church faithful to its head cannot long abide in the mansions of affluence.

> Many Christians have recently been becoming more and more aware that if the church wants to be faithful to the God of Jesus Christ, it has to rethink itself from below, from the position of the poor of this world, the exploited classes, the despised races, the marginal cultures. It must descend into the world's hells and commune with poverty, injustice, the struggles and hopes of the dispossessed because of them is the kingdom of Heaven. Basically it means the church living as a church the way many of its own members live as human beings. Being reborn as a church means dying to a history of oppression and complicity. Its power to live anew depends on whether it has the courage to die. This is its passover. . . . The aim is to be faithful to the gospel, and the constant renewal of God's call. Gradually people are realizing that in the last resort, it is not a question of the church being poor, but of the poor of this world being the people of God, the disturbing witness, of the God who sets free.[4]

4. Gustavo Gutierrez, "The Poor in the Church" in *The Poor and the Church*, edited by Norbert Greinacher and Alois Muller (New York: Seabury Press, 1977), p. 13.

One may agree or disagree with some of the theology or practice of liberation theology, but it is difficult to argue with the notion that the church is not intended to be another institution at the bidding of the rich and powerful.

When Karl Marx declared that religion was the "opiate of the people," he was largely reflecting what he saw. The church, by promising people heaven in the future, helped keep them content with nothing in the present. It was simply one more oppressive power, helping to prop up the rich and powerful.

But the church must not speak for the privileged; its voice must be raised instead on behalf of the oppressed. It is not a political weapon for the powerful but the voice of God for the weak.

This is without question a difficult area of the church's mission. What tactics should the church employ to bring about a world that more closely reflects God's desires? There are at least three different levels of possible involvement. The first is persuasion. Here the church goes to the streets and attempts to win commitment from others to the values of the kingdom by preaching. The second is political. At this level the church attempts to use the political process to establish institutions congenial to the values of the kingdom. The third is revolution or civil disobedience, where the church feels compelled to go beyond the regular political apparatus for more radical solutions.

Although almost everyone would agree that the first level is appropriate, there is wide divergence on the latter two. These will ultimately have to be left up to the consciences of individual Christians.

But the church's proclamation of justice and holiness and righteousness has credibility only when it is exhibited in the life of the church itself. The church must proclaim righteousness in her life. There are three conspicuous areas in which this must be done.

First, in the church there is no room for elitism of any sort. God's vision for the church is that there be neither rich nor poor, black nor white, male nor female. The privilege of power and position has no place in the church.

> My brothers, as believers in our glorious Lord Jesus Christ, don't show favoritism. Suppose a man comes into your meeting wearing a gold ring and fine clothes, and a poor man in shabby clothes also comes in. If you show special attention to the man wearing fine clothes and say "Here's a good seat for you," but say to the poor man, "You stand there" or "Sit on the floor at my feet," have you not discriminated among yourselves and become judges with evil thoughts? . . .
> If you really keep the royal law found in scripture, "Love your neighbor as yourself," you are doing right. But if you show favoritism, you sin (Jas. 2:1-4, 8-9).

In a world that caters to beauty, wealth, and power, the church resists and refuses to be drawn into this worldliness. Fair play and respect for all mark its relations. It is a sad fact of history that many American churches were dragged kicking and screaming into integration in the 1960s. The church should be the leader in the practice of mutual respect and integrity and justice. The church should set the moral tone for her society.

It is an equally distressing fact that even today there are some congregations where the poor do not feel welcome. The church is not the church when society's outcasts are not as comfortable as the culture's elite.

Second, the church must steer away from becoming a "power institution." That is, among the institutions of this world, the church as Christ's body seeks only spiritual influence, not financial or social prominence. The church must not be enticed by power. The church is in the world not to dominate but to serve. The world has seen enough of institutions corrupted by power and money. The church cannot claim to be the vanguard of the kingdom of God and behave like the kingdoms of this world. Perhaps it is time for the church to take a vow of poverty in imitation of her master who had no place to lay his head. It is time for the church to be crucified with Christ, to lay down her life for people rather than asking people to give all to her.

It will be particularly difficult for large congregations to avoid the mentality and practice of multi-million-dollar corporations, but this is not at the heart of being a church. The church has no legitimate interests other than holiness and righteousness. The church cannot call the world to these realities while hopelessly entangled in the affairs of the world.

Third, the church must practice discipline among its own. It will not do to have the church screaming at the sins of the world while its own members sin with impunity. Church discipline is not popular today, but it is essential to the proclamation of the kingdom.

Church discipline does not mean trying to weed out all the sinners from the church, lest we altogether empty our churches, nor does it mean kicking out those who commit particularly offensive sins in order to protect a certain image. It does mean that each of us has the responsibility to lovingly but seriously call those around us to holy living—and that each of us has the obligation to be responsive to that call. This process is neither arrogant nor mean. Those seeking to live under the reign of God are always ready to respond to correction.

There will always be some who refuse to accept the demands of the kingdom. The church must regretfully recognize them as part of the world, but this will be the exception among a group of people who cultivate holiness. The church must become a center of moral and spiritual value and be unapologetic in its stand for righteousness.

So the church not only proclaims the righteousness of God and calls the world to holiness and justice, it exhibits that presence of the kingdom in its midst. It does so by welcoming all, disdaining worldly power and prominence, and practicing holy discipline among its members.

Prophetic Aspect

The final part of the church's mission is the prophetic aspect. Theologically, this means that the church refuses to identify itself or its culture with the kingdom of God in any absolute way. Churches must never merely reflect the values of the nation or culture of which they are a part. They also must stand against those values as something less than the divine holiness.

This may seem obvious enough, especially when the church finds itself in the midst of an openly hostile and antagonistic environment. When, for instance, the government is overtly atheistic and engaged in militant persecution of the church, God's people must certainly stand against this kind of opposition. But even when government and culture are friendly, the church must beware because these things are finally only human. American Christians and churches have proven to be particularly susceptible to confusing the kingdom of God and its goals with the aspirations of the United States.

The prophetic ministry is the task of proclaiming the judgment of God against every human enterprise because all such efforts are both finite and, at least somewhat, willful. The church cannot allow people to place their trust in the goodness and accomplishments of their culture, nation, or even the church itself. The victories of these are always only partial, falling short of divine perfection. So ultimate trust can finally be placed only in God's grace expressed in Christ—not in a culture, nation, or church. Bringing this truth constantly to awareness is central to the church's mission.

As the prophet wrote long ago:

> This is what the Lord says:
> "Let not the wise man boast of his wisdom
> or the strong man boast of his strength
> or the rich man boast of his riches,
> but let him who boasts boast about this:
> that he understands and knows me,
> that I am the Lord, who exercises kindness,
> justice, and righteousness on earth,
> for in these I delight,"
> declares the Lord (Jer. 9:23-24).

Dare we fail to point out here that the modern church is in danger of idolatry? If we fail to heed the prophetic warning against boasting of self and trusting in human accomplishments, we will become idolaters of the first order. Although the issue of idolatry is often thought of in terms of Baal worship or child sacrifice, it truly is an issue of contemporary significance as well. Modern man has in no sense eluded its lure. Perhaps Paul Tillich has best identified what is at stake. In distinguishing between "true faith" and "idolatrous faith," he wrote:

> In true faith the ultimate concern is a concern about the truly ultimate; while in idolatrous faith preliminary, finite realities are elevated to the rank of ultimacy.[5]

---

5. Paul Tillich, *The Dynamics of Faith* (New York: Harper & Row, 1957), p. 12.

In Tillich's terms, idolatry occurs when humans place their trust in something other than ultimate reality—God. It is as true of our day as that of the prophet that we are tempted to place our trust in our riches or our strength or our wisdom. There is, of course, nothing wrong with any of these things in themselves. They are all capable of being used to God's glory. Cultures and societies take understandable and justifiable pride in the material things they create for their citizens, in the educational, artistic, and scientific achievements of their schools and universities, and of their armies and technologies that protect their accomplishments. But, when these finite and passing things are given the halo of ultimacy, they become idolatrous.

While the church does not belittle human achievement, it must be quick to point out that this is all it is—*human* achievement. The nation passes away, but God endures. Abundance is followed by drought and financial booms by recessions and depressions, but God endures. Great cultures collapse, philosophical systems change, and yesterday's truth is tomorrow's discarded theory, but God endures.

The most sinister of all idolatries is religion itself, leading to Karl Barth's famous lament "religion is the great enemy of God." The church must constantly take care to distinguish "faith in religion" from "faith in God."

Consider as an example Jeremiah's famous sermon:

> Do not trust in deceptive words and say,
> "This is the temple of the Lord, the temple of
> the Lord, the temple of the Lord!" . . . Will you
> steal and murder, commit adultery and per-
> jury, burn incense to Baal and follow other
> gods you have not known, and then come and
> stand before me in this house which bears my
> Name, and say, "We are safe"—safe to do all
> these detestable things? . . . Therefore, what I
> did to Shiloh I will now do to the house that
> bears my Name, the temple you trust in . . . I
> will thrust you from my presence (Jer. 7:1-15).

Notice the shift that had taken place in the object
of trust. Their trust was no longer in God but the
temple. Their trust was in a particular manifestation of God's presence and a particular kind of
human expression of religion, not in the transcendent God.

To say it another way, the church must constantly guard against becoming the object of its
own faith. Only God deserves that. The church
must not confuse itself with God. Loyalty to a particular denomination may replace loyalty to God.

Have you ever thought about the fact that, for
some people, a relationship with God is virtually
synonymous with church activity? If the particular
religious community of which they are a part were
to disappear tomorrow, for them it would amount
to the disappearance of God. *The church is not God.*

Religious traditions rise and wane, but God remains. The church must prophetically proclaim
this truth. So whenever man aspires to deity,

whether his pretension be materialistic, nationalistic, scientific, humanist, or religionist, the church always proclaims, these are *not* God.

Conclusion

The mission of the church is never merely the perpetuation of an institution but the continuation of the work of Christ. Joseph Comblin suggests that there are two radically different ways of viewing gospel mission. The first is ecclesiocentric.

> The first way views this mission as the expansion and increase of the groups that are visibly integrated into the institutional forms of the existing church. Missionary activity comes down to recruiting new members into the church, increasing the adherents, and adding to its prestige and social influence. The spoken word is used to argue, convince, and attract people to the church.[6]

The second view of mission is Christocentric.

> The second view of the Gospel mission does not start with the church but rather with Christ himself. It sees the Gospel mission as an imitation and renewal of his mission . . . Jesus addressed himself to those who were outside. He spoke to denounce and announce, to provoke a transformation in people's lives, to liberate people from the dead weight of the

6. Joseph Comblin, *The Meaning of Mission*, translated by John Drury (Maryknoll, NY: Orbis Book, 1977), p. 9.

> past, the synagogue, the scribes, and the tra-
> ditional outlook. The church comes after the
> Gospel mission, not before it. The privileged
> objects of the Gospel mission are the lost
> sheep: publicans, sinners, prostitutes, lowly
> Galileans, and many other of that ilk.[7]

There may be no greater threat to the accomplishment of the real mission of the church than its
diversion to the pseudo-mission indicated above. It
is axiomatic that all institutions attempt to perpetuate themselves, but the church errs greatly when
it sees the expansion of its own influence as the ultimate goal. The church partakes in a transcendent
reality, but it is not that reality. The church seeks
not its own glory but the glory of God. It behaves
not as a typical human institution but as the body
of Christ.

The church's mission is to model transcendent
living to the world. It does this not by escape from
the world but by living in it. By demonstrating a
love beyond the human. By calling for holiness anchored in the very nature of God. By proclaiming
the need for divine grace without which every cultural and religious achievement comes to naught.
When the church faithfully executes this mission,
it displays the transcendent realities of the Spirit.
The church does not denigrate the world and culture because they are passing away, for this world
is the arena of God's glory. Rather, the church ele-
vates every task in the world as an offering to the
One who is All in All.

---

7. Comblin, *Meaning of Mission*, pp. 10-11.

CHAPTER NINE

Evangelism:
The Seeking Church

Until the Lord Jesus Christ returns to receive his redeemed church to himself, the mission of that church will revolve around faithful proclamation of the gospel. Just as it was at Corinth in the first century, the redemptive story of the death, burial, and resurrection of Christ is still the matter of "first importance" (1 Cor. 15:3-4).

If we understand *evangelism* to be the responsibility of the Christian community to bear witness to the saving work of God in Christ, the task of this chapter is to outline an incarnational model for doing so in the new century. Our thesis here is that the church's evangelistic task is to disclose Jesus to people for the sake of making possible a life-changing encounter.

Before moving on, it is imperative that this thesis statement be understood and taken seriously. It is meant to be a humbler statement of the church's evangelistic task than is typically offered. *We do* not confront the world. *We* do not convert the world. *We* do not save the world. Our total contribution to the salvation task is to make possible an event of encounter between Jesus and lost people. Appealing to Paul's words again, the evangelistic work of the church is neither to exhibit "superior wisdom" nor "persuasive words" but to hold forth "Jesus Christ and him crucified" (1 Cor. 2:1-5).

At the start of the story of Jesus is the truth of the incarnation. "The Word became flesh" in the infant of Bethlehem. Infinite love was lived out in finite flesh. By means of the incarnation, we now know the meaning of grace, truth, and forgiveness. These once-abstract notions were given flesh-and-blood reality in his person.

At the start of the story of the church is the truth of a second incarnation. God's Word must be enfleshed again and again in communities of faith. The presence and power of the Spirit of God must be visible in the lives of people who know Jesus. We must "flesh out" the meaning of grace, truth, and forgiveness in the church. In our one-to-one relationships with unbelievers, we must give substance to these qualities. Thus we will provide the opportunity for Christ to encounter them, bring them to repentance, and save them.

This is a "humbler" statement of our evangelistic task because it puts the burden for salvation where it has always belonged. While God has graciously chosen to allow us to participate in the process of salvation as heralds of good news, he reserves both redemption and judgment for himself. This understanding is not only more biblical, it is better for us in purely practical terms. It helps us avoid the tendency to reduce our evangelism to number-oriented programs which are more like search-and-destroy operations than anything resembling Christ's presence in the world.

"Evangelizing the world" is therefore understood in this attempt at 21st-century ecclesiology to focus on what God has done, not on what we need to do. Today's results-centered evangelism is different from the New Testament paradigm of Christ-centered evangelism. Although Paul was sensitive in his approach to people (cf. 1 Cor. 9:19-23), he never placed the desire for a favorable hearing for his message above his commitment to preaching Christ faithfully. His strategy was rooted instead in his commitment to a faithful statement of the joy-bringing thing God had done in history through Jesus of Nazareth. He declared that God had done in Christ what he had promised through the prophets. He proclaimed that the needs of all mankind had been met through this one event. This was—and is—the gospel.

A faithful church must take its cue for evangelism from New Testament precedent rather than imitating the successful marketing scheme of a "soul-winning church" that has adopted a methodology without explicit focus on the death, burial, and resurrection of Jesus. Weight-loss programs, youth retreats, and charismatic pulpit presence may provide a context for a faithful proclamation of the gospel. On the other hand, they may combine to build a large and successful religious enterprise whose identity is defined by something very different from the gospel.

Recent church history is filled with instances of personality-centered or program-centered movements which had phenomenal success in the short term. With the central person gone, personality-centered movements tend to collapse. Program-centered movements invariably become rigid legalisms in which the maintenance of "the program" dominates all other concerns. Neither is consistent with the sort of evangelism that gives "first importance" to Christ's finished work at the cross.

Before examining three elements of the church's evangelistic work, we must first examine the convictions which underlie biblical evangelism. Once clear about the foundation, we can move directly to clarify the task itself.

Convictions That Underlie Evangelism

First, human lives apart from God are intellectually misguided, morally ambiguous, and spiritually dead. When our society speaks of success and "the good life," it most often defines them in terms of what we have and where we are. These concepts rarely point to who we are. And they carefully sidestep anything that relates to God, Scripture, or eternity. So it becomes important for people to remain youthful, trim, and well-groomed. These are the keys to a pleasure-seeking lifestyle. Women must be beautiful to be desirable, and men must be athletic and well-heeled to catch them.

Power and popularity are also critical to success in America. All of us know their symbols: titles, office size, salary, and invitations to the right events hosted by the right people. That Vanna White and

Madonna are better known to our children than Mother Teresa is a sad commentary on our values.

Then there is the compulsion to produce, to achieve, to get results. The person who gets ahead is the one whose productivity this quarter outstrips last quarter—again and again. So the pressure is on to steal an account or to do something unethical to make a profit. Lies are told. Figures are juggled. Family and friends are betrayed.

Finally, of course, comes the real yardstick of "the good life"—money—or at least the appearance of money. A big house, a fancy car, expensive clothes, membership in the right clubs, and vacations to the chic spots are measurements of success. In the 1987 movie *Wall Street,* Michael Douglas, playing the dollar-thirsty takeover specialist Gordon Gekko, gives a frighteningly realistic speech:

> Greed is good. Greed is right. Greed works. Greed clarifies, cuts through and captures the essence of the evolutionary spirit. Greed—in all of its forms—greed of life, for money, for love, knowledge, has marked the upward surge of mankind, and greed, you mark my words, will not only save Teldar Paper but that other malfunctioning corporation called the USA.

Please don't conclude that the Bible teaches that youth, health, popularity, and money are evil. Not one of them is judged. Not a single one of them is evil. But to define human worth in terms of any or all of them is evil. To live one's life in pursuit of one or more of them to the neglect of God, relationships, family, or integrity is evil. To sacrifice the greater things possible for us in this life for a handful of trinkets is foolish. To sell a soul for the fool's gold of this life is to make a poor deal.

Anyone who knows the intellectual history of the 20th century is not surprised that we have evolved a society which abounds in broken promises, greed, chemical dependency, divorce, sexual perversion, and crime. The logical positivism, pragmatism, and existentialism of the first half of the twentieth century elbowed themselves into the public consciousness with "scientific pronouncements" concerning the meaninglessness of metaphysics, God, and morality. Truth became relative, and the scientific method became the sole arbiter of objectivity. Ethical norms were tossed out the window. Individual freedom became the only absolute. Everyone was left to do as he or she pleased, and the remainder of society was supposed to find its nobility through tolerance of whatever followed— sexual license, the drug culture, and so on.

This recent intellectual history is the outworking of the spirit of the Enlightenment. At the start of the 18th century, this movement began to replace divine revelation with human reason, God with nature, and religion with science. The world became a closed system and miracles were confined to a "prescientific" era. The Bible became a book to be interpreted as a collection of myths expressing a particular insight into the nature of things. Historic Christianity fell victim to secular humanism in the public mind.

The *Oxford English Dictionary* defines "secularism" as the notion that morality should be based solely on regard for the well-being of humankind in this present life to the exclusion of all considerations related to belief in God or a future life. Secular humanism makes humankind the norm of all truth and value. The idea of a transcendent deity or an eternal and absolute standard of right and wrong is ridiculed. Entertainers, educators, legislators, scientists, theologians, musicians, writers—people from all spheres of influence can be cited who are aggressive advocates of the nontheistic perspective on life. The foundations of our culture have been shaken by their combined leadership.

From the rebellion of the original pair against God, this cycle of shutting out God, pursuing a self-willed course for life, and suffering the inevitable consequences has repeated itself again and again. Paul described it in an epistle he wrote during the seventh decade of the first Christian century.

> So I tell you this, and insist on it in the Lord, that you must no longer live as the Gentiles do, in the futility of their thinking. They are darkened in their understanding and separated from the life of God because of the ignorance that is in them due to the hardening of their hearts. Having lost all sensitivity, they have given themselves over to sensuality so as to indulge in every kind of impurity, with a continual lust for more (Eph. 4:17-19; cf. Rom. 1:18ff).

In a word, humans need the gospel because of
sin. Lost and bewildered, we cannot find our way
out of the intellectual, moral, and spiritual darkness we have created by shutting out the light of
God's presence.

Second, the gospel alone addresses and satisfies
the human need for truth grounded in historical reality. Our modern thought-world is cluttered with
trivial, false, and dangerous messages. There is
New Age jargon which resurrects old pagan notions
of astrology, reincarnation, and self-deification.
There are Eastern religions by the dozens. Then
one finds a host of left-wing "Christian" groups
that make no distinctive claim for Jesus of
Nazareth and embrace the goal of harmonizing all
religious traditions into one all-embracing religion.
Over against them are many right-wing
"Christian" groups that have entrenched themselves in legalistic battling over relatively insignificant issues while ignoring such major issues as justice, racism, and hunger.

Because of these aberrations from historical
Christianity, secularism's depiction of all religion
has credibility. Thinking people have developed a
deep distrust of Christian "evangelism" because of
the unscrupulous televangelists or churches they
know which specialize in cheap promotional tactics
and psychological manipulation in the name of
"evangelizing the lost." The only hope for reaching
these people is a responsible presentation of the
historic Christian message.

Against the exaltation of reason over revelation
and the tendency of many to subjectivize Scripture

into triviality, the church must proclaim the historic Christ on the basis of a trustworthy Bible. The Gospel writers were not advancing their personal insights via myth. They recorded history and invited their readers to believe in the person who was the focus of their record. The mighty acts of God in Christ were seen as bringing to fulfillment the divine promise of human redemption which had been originated in Eden (Gen. 3:15), were later affirmed to Abraham (Gen. 12:2-3), and then were certified to the nation of Israel (Deut 18:15-18).

Scripture does indeed reflect the various cultures in which it was produced. It also exhibits the inevitable dilemma of putting divine revelation into human language. This is why historical and literary criticism are valuable tools in its interpretation, for the *goal* of our interpretive process is to uncover the unique truth of God's entrance into history. We do not subscribe to the view that Scripture is simply a powerful literary presentation of the human condition that has little to do with actual events in space and time.

Take the third Gospel as a case in point. Luke was not an eyewitness to the life of Christ. He had learned what he knew of Jesus from the apostles and other eyewitnesses to his life. As an educated and free man, however, he did not accept what he was told uncritically. He investigated for himself, visited critical sites, and interrogated people who had first-hand knowledge of the man from Nazareth. Only then, with his own mind assured on the matter, did he draw up an account of the life, teaching, and significance of Jesus Christ.

Thus his Gospel opens:

> Many have undertaken to draw up an ac-
> count of the things that have been fulfilled
> among us, just as they were handed down to
> us by those who from the first were eyewit-
> nesses and servants of the word. Therefore,
> since I myself have carefully investigated ev-
> erything from the beginning, it seemed good
> also to me to write an orderly account for you,
> most excellent Theophilus, so that you may
> know the certainty of the things you have
> been taught (Luke 1:1-4).

If language means anything, it is certain that
Luke was not attempting to couch a particular
world view in the language of nonhistorical fabrica-
tion. He was writing a factual account of things
"fulfilled among us"; he was concerned to establish
for Theophilus the "certainty" of the things he had
learned about Jesus.

Against the interpretation of Christianity as a
private, subjective experience for simple-minded
people, we must present the truth that God actually entered history in the person of Jesus.
Against the New Age Movement, Eastern cults,
and right- or left-wing parodies of true religion,
the 21st-century church must bear faithful witness to the biblical message of God's saving work
in Christ. We must enter the arena of human
thought to challenge post-Enlightenment prejudices against God, truth, and holiness.

Several texts in the book of Acts point to a
Pauline method of evangelism which appealed to

the distinctive truthfulness of the message about Christ. Paul "reasoned with" the Jews of Thessalonica concerning the messiahship of Jesus of Nazareth (Acts 17:2). When he entered Athens, a center for philosophy and scholarship in his time, he "reasoned in the synagogue with the Jews and God-fearing Greeks, as well as in the marketplace day by day with those who happened to be there" (Acts 17:17). Unlike the myths of Homer and Hesiod, the core truths of Christianity are space-time events with eternal significance. The very historicity of our faith makes it unique and compelling. Against the modern tendency of translating the gospel into psychobabble designed to stimulate self-awareness and human potentiation, we insist that the only worthy way to present the gospel is to offer it as the objectively truthful account of what God has done in history to save men and women who are the objects of his love.

Third, the gospel, and the gospel alone, satisfies the needs that we have by consensus labelled "ultimate" in human experience. It has just been protested that some misrepresent the Christian message as a psychologically helpful story without regard to its truthfulness. It would be equally appropriate to inveigh against those who lecture and debate on behalf of the historicity of Scripture without making clear its dynamic power to both orient and anchor the human spirit and to change the course of a misdirected life. Part of the proof of Christianity's divine origin and truthfulness is tied to its ability to satisfy the deepest needs of humanity.

Several paragraphs ago, we reflected on what moderns have come to think of as "the good life." The point then was that such a lifestyle is a busy distraction from God. People can fill their time in pursuit of pleasure, titles, and money in order to crowd God out of their conscious minds. Humans make themselves the measure of all things. Thus preoccupied with never-satisfied aspirations, many survive for a lifetime with only a vague sense that something is missing. In those moments of faint uneasiness, they surely tell themselves that their discomfort traces to the fact that they have not yet realized some current preoccupation. Thus they move from one obsession to another without realizing that the problem is not with the expenditure of energy but with the Christless objects of their pursuit.

The person who is most likely to despair, however, is the one who *does* attain all the goals. She rises to the absolute summit of career or profession. He makes enough money that his financial security is guaranteed. He becomes the most famous personality of his generation. The despair surfaces in the fact that success, applause, and money don't make a person happy. The striver can make himself believe that his unhappiness is due to unrealized ambition; the person who actually realizes all her fantasies is confused that it doesn't satisfy. "Is this it?" comes the lament. Bizarre behaviors, chemical dependency, and suicide among people who attain what most people envy witness to the failure of anything on earth to give ultimate fulfillment.

Three thousand years ago, the wealthiest, wisest, and most pleasure-sated king who had ever lived surveyed his achievements apart from God and said, "Utterly meaningless! Everything is meaningless" (Eccl. 1:2b). Others who have attained their own version of his success have cried the same bitter tears. "In this world there are only two tragedies," wrote Oscar Wilde. "One is not getting what one wants, and the other is getting it."[1] The latter is unquestionably the worse fate for the person who does not know Christ.

The human spirit naturally looks for meaning to existence, longs for home, turns toward God. After challenging the pagan notion of God (i.e., he "does not live in temples built by hands"), Paul went on to explain the Christian concept of God. Instead of being "served by human hands, as if he needed anything," the God in whom Christians believe "gives all men life and breath and everything else." He alone is self-sufficient and eternal, the creator of all mankind who has set the possibilities and limits of our world. "God did this so that men would seek him and perhaps reach out for him and find him, though he is not far from each one of us" (Acts 17:24-27). Summarized by Augustine, "Thou hast created us for thyself, and our hearts cannot be satisfied until they find rest in thee."[2]

At the close of the 20th century, a phenomenon was witnessed by both church leaders and sociologists. A generation that had been influenced and

---

1. Quoted in Harold Kushner, *When All You've Ever Wanted Isn't Enough* (New York: Pocket Books, 1986) p. 16.
2. *Confessions*. 1. 1.

guided by secularism to reject spiritual themes was passionately seeking after spirituality. The much-discussed "baby boomers"—generally understood as those born between 1946 and 1964—were seeking after God. At one time or another, approximately two-thirds of baby boomers had dropped out of organized religion. Yet by 1990, more than one-third of the dropouts had returned. More than 80 percent of them reported themselves to be "religious" and said they believed in life after death. The largest group of returnees were couples with children.[3] While some of these seekers settled for an unnamed Higher Power, a New Age guru, or some other substitute, the search itself was prompted by their nature as creatures in God's own image. The full satisfaction of such spiritual needs can be found only in Christ.

Every life needs meaning. Is there a larger purpose for which I am doing all these daily tasks? Is there any reason for me to be honest when others are not? How do I prioritize the things pressing for my time? "But seek first his kingdom and his righteousness, and all these things will be given to you as well" (Matt. 6:33). The kingdom life (i.e., life under the sovereign rule of God) really is the best life. It has depth of conviction and breadth of vision. Even the most trivial event of life has meaning as it is done or reacted to by faith.

Every life needs love. "How great is the love the Father has lavished on us, that we should be called children of God!" wrote John. "And that is what we

3. Statistics from Kenneth L. Woodward *et al.*, "A Time to Seek," *Newsweek* (Dec. 17, 1990), pp. 50-56.

are!" (1 John 3:1a). To hear the story of the gospel is to understand the real meaning of love. It is self-giving, self-sacrificing action on behalf of another. Anyone who sees Christ's cross through the eye of faith knows that he or she is loved beyond measure.

Every life needs security for the sake of growth through struggle. "And we know that in all things God works for the good of those who love him, who have been called according to his purpose" (Rom. 8:28). This verse does not attribute everything that happens in a given human life to the hand of God. He gives good gifts (Jas. 1:17), but much of life is ugly and hateful. Temptation, discouragement, evil—these are not the inventions and bequests of God. They are Satan's typical means of destroying us. Paul's affirmation in Romans 8:28 is that in all things—even those that were intended by Satan to hurt us—God will work with us to bring a good result. He will support and strengthen, bring hope from despair, give victory in what appears to be defeat.

Every life longs to survive death, to live eternally. Jesus' own triumph over death is the assurance that we too will live forever. "Christ has indeed been raised from the dead, the firstfruits of those who have fallen asleep" (1 Cor. 15:20).

These presuppositions constitute a foundation for evangelism. If they are not believed, what motive could there be for wanting to share the gospel? If they are believed, what could restrain one from sharing it?

The Church's Work of Evangelism

As the church seeks to be faithful to its evangelistic role in the world, there are three critical
tasks before us in the 21st century.

First, faithful evangelism must be rooted in the
church's role of *being Christ to the world*. This is simply to affirm that before we have the right to *say*
anything to people around us, we must first *be* something to them. We must take seriously the idea that
the church is a second incarnation of the Eternal
Word. We must be Christ's presence in the world.
The Word must be enfleshed again through us.

The Body of Christ is not called by its head to
monasticism but to "sacred secularity." We are led
by Christ's own example to live in earthly communities with a heavenly commitment. We serve him
by serving the people about us, and we serve the
people about us by exhibiting and declaring the
values we know in him.

Two equally fatal errors render us impotent. On
the one hand, some Christians are so concerned
about the world to come that they are no good to
anybody in this one. On the other hand, some get
so caught up in ministering to this world that they
forget to keep their focus on a goal that lies outside
it. The challenge is for the church to live heavenly
truth so faithfully that it makes a worldly difference. Peace, justice, homelessness, ethics in government, racism, AIDS, abortion—all these issues
of concern to our time must be of concern to the
church. If Jesus died for people whose lives are affected by these problems, we cannot turn away
from them. As with Jesus and the woman of

Samaria, our right to speak to these people about "living water" will likely begin with our sharing a cup of cold water from some well of earthly resources.

More often than not, however, we begin our attempts at sharing Christ with words rather than deeds. A church wants to "get evangelistic," so someone leads a pep rally urging everyone to be conscious of lost souls, to pray for their salvation, and to watch for the right moment to share the gospel with them. There may be a flush of enthusiasm. There may even be a few people saved. But the program typically runs out of steam rather quickly and has to be jump-started again in a few months. It happens because we are going out to make "cold calls" on neighbors we don't really know, recent visitors to our services, or mates of our members. We bump into resistance. There is even skepticism about our motives. And it seldom works.

It shouldn't surprise us that this sort of evangelistic "program" falls flat. For one thing, it is intrusive in its nature. It involves barging into someone's life, setting up a Bible study, and attempting to achieve a conversion. (How do you like to have Mormon elders or Jehovah's Witnesses ring your doorbell and interrupt your time at home with your family?) For another, it has no background of love, integrity, and credibility. Your "prospect" doesn't know you, has no reason to trust you, and has no experience of Christ through you.

During Jesus' public ministry, he ate with sinners, made outcasts feel comfortable, and broke all manner of rabbinic traditions in order to help peo-

ple. He saw himself in the world to minister healing to those whose lives were broken (cf. Luke 4:16-
21). When we become a second incarnation, we will
be among the same people doing the same healing
things he did.

When Ultimate Wisdom, Ultimate Love, and
Ultimate Hope became flesh and lived among us,
he executed the divine plan to make himself understood through a very simple strategy. He did not
found an evangelistic organization and travel from
city to city on fund-raising tours. He did not found
an orphanage. He did not open a hospital. He did
not call a press conference to reveal his identity
through some astounding display of miraculous
power.

What did he do? He lived among the people as
one of them. He embodied the gospel message in
his person. He acted. He demonstrated his message
by his life before setting about to explain it with
his words. "Too much talk and too little action"
could easily be the indictment of the modern
church. Our teaching is often ineffective because it
fails to offer a life-based example of what we are offering. We have let lifeless words take the place of
enfleshed wisdom, love, and hope. A lost world is
not rushing to hear our sermons; it is waiting to
see our demonstration of the gospel message in
flesh-and-blood performance.

Religion as most of us know it often isolates us
from the world. Jesus went to the world, loved the
world, and saved the world. Our church buildings
and programs can get in the way of our involvement
in that mission unless we are very careful.

Being members of today's typical church can serve to insulate us from pain. Yet Jesus took the pains of others to himself and bore their burdens. Are we to protect ourselves from the things he embraced? If we serve our Lord in this world, it will have to be through ministering to some of his least brothers (cf. Matt. 25:40,45).

Our practice of religion sometimes winds up hurting people who have already been hurt too much. For example, it sometimes creates a sense of greater guilt instead of a sense of relief. Tax collectors and prostitutes left the presence of Jesus unburdened. Guilty, penitent people sometimes come to our most conservative churches only to be scolded, censured, and made to feel worse; they go to the most liberal ones only to be reassured with what they know is a hollow lie which tells them they are already accepted in their aberrant lifestyle. Where is the gentle, compassionate presence of the Christ who could still speak boldly of repentance, give hope without compromising with sin, and love the sinner while hating his sin?

While acting as the salt of the earth to touch, penetrate, and purify the world with Christ's presence, the church must also be a community of light. It must be a cross-centered society where heaven's version of truth and life is given precedence over the world's. It is a body fully aware of its own sinfulness and living in the joyous liberation of forgiveness. Its members tell the truth, love their enemies, and respect the outcast. It is a beehive of good works that resemble Christ's own compassionate involvement with human pain. Its people love worship, for it clarifies anew their vision of God and recreates their experience of encounter with him through Christ.

First published almost a century and a half ago, the following story was told of a missionary to the Seneca Indians by the name of Cram. He spoke to a council of chiefs and warriors of the Six Nations at Buffalo Creek, New York, in the presence of the United States Agent for Indian Affairs in the summer of 1805. Said the missionary:

> I am come, brethren, to enlighten your minds, and to instruct you how to worship the Great Spirit agreeably to his will, and to preach to you the gospel of his Son, Jesus Christ. There is but one way to serve God, and if you do not embrace the right way, you cannot be happy hereafter.

To his offer, the Seneca chiefs replied:

> Brother, we understand your religion is written in a Book. You say there is but one way to worship and serve the Great Spirit. If there is but one religion, why do you white people differ so much about it? Why not all agree, as you can all read the book? Brother, we do not understand these things.
>
> We are also told your religion was given to your forefathers. We also have a religion which was given to our forefathers. It teaches us to be thankful for all the favors we receive, to love one another, and to be united. We never quarrel about religion.

We are told you have been preaching to the white people in this place. Those people are our neighbors; we are acquainted with them. We will wait a little, to see what effect your preaching has upon them. If we find it does them good, makes them honest and less disposed to cheat Indians, we will then consider again what you have said.[4]

The non-Christians' expectation that the church show them something of Christ's transforming presence before presuming to speak in his name is not unreasonable. We must learn to exhibit unity in Christ. We must find a way to forego rancor and quarreling about our denominational traditions. We must accept our high calling to live as men and women of personal integrity. We must disclose that God is with us in our families, jobs, and conversations.

Second, evangelism speaks to *the insufficiency of this world* to satisfy humankind's deepest needs. Without reviewing all that has been said earlier on this point, this part of the church's evangelistic task involves a method comparable to holding a mirror before the world's collective face.

True to Nietzsche's prophecy, our culture has killed God, dug his grave, and built churches that are his tombs and sepulchers. Yet, still following Nietzsche, there remain people who are the equivalent of his "madman" who stand in the marketplace in the glare of the bright morning hours, holding a lantern and crying incessantly, "I seek God! I seek God!"

4. A. Campbell, "Disciples of Christ, Christians, Reformers. No. I: Supplement" in *Millennial Harbinger* (April 1854): 198-199.

There are contemporary "prophets" who speak to the situation of our world apart from God. Just as Paul quoted the Old Testament to the Jews but Greek poets to the philosophers on the Areopagus, we must be wise enough to make contact with people of our time through the music, plays, novels, and films they know. Nothing speaks quite so quickly to modern man. If someone knows Nietzsche, begin with Nietzsche. Perhaps the point of contact will be Paul Simon, Solzhenitsyn, or George Will. Whenever you hear a biblical theme addressed, there is a potential opening for discussion with an unbeliever. Just as a missionary or business person in a foreign culture must learn the local language in order to be effective, so must Christians who are aliens on earth know its intellectual, cultural, and artistic vocabulary.

In the course of those conversations, listen for particular points of contact with each person. It may be her fear of death or his sense of moral failure. It may be a pervasive sense of loneliness or meaninglessness. Listen with genuine interest when these issues surface. Take the person seriously, and try to understand why his or her worldview is inadequate to address the problem.

If this sounds too simple and makes you think that all we are suggesting at this point is developing friendships, you are getting the point. The average Christian tends to have few non-Christian friends. Although we work, attend classes, car pool, and exchange pleasantries with unbelievers, we typically make few friends outside the circle of faith. Of course there are biblical passages about withdrawal from the world. God demands that we avoid compromise with the evils of this world, and he wants our fellowship with his other children to be meaningful and special. From this it does not follow, however, that we are justified in isolating ourselves from non-Christians.

Looking again to our paradigm, Jesus was contemporary with the Pharisees. They were a segregated and isolated fellowship within the larger body of both Judaism and the larger world. Jesus did not adopt their methodology. He was a friend to sinners and moved freely among the very people the Pharisees took care to avoid. He made them feel comfortable in his presence, and he led them into the kingdom of God. We should learn Jesus' approach to unsaved people, not that of the Pharisees.

Hospitality, neighborliness, and friendship are Bible words and concepts. One of the requirements of an elder is hospitality (1 Tim. 3:2), and all believers are exhorted to "entertain strangers" (Heb. 13:2). Caring about people very different from oneself is what the Parable of the Good Samaritan is about. Friendship with a lost person is the first step in breaking down the barrier which is presently keeping him from hearing about Christ.

Build bridges of communication with non-Christians in your world. Open your home and family life to include people who are not believers. Be hospitable and outgoing with them. Build on your common interests, hobbies, or family situation. Be sensitive to their needs, and be the first person there to offer real help in any time of crisis.

Evangelism is really a way of life rather than a project. Do you want to be someone's "project" or a name on his "prospect list"? We seriously doubt that your neighbor wants to be thought of in those terms either. Friendship, one writer said, is "the language the deaf can hear and the blind can see." It is the language Christians must speak.

In the course of such relationships, gently drive home the point of the world's spiritual bankruptcy while exhibiting the richness of genuine faith. With tact and sensitivity, challenge the unbeliever to see both the presuppositions and logical extensions of his worldview. Avoid being contentious and ill-natured, but when possible help people see that without Christ there is an inevitable void in life.

The vague sense of ache that arises in the souls of men and women who begin to see the poverty of their non-Christian worldviews is simply their longing for God. It cannot be filled with toys or success, fame or education, noise or flickering images. The mess we have made of our world has placed more and more people on a quest for the sacred in a society that was only recently boasting of its liberation from God. The post-Vietnam, post-Watergate, post-Boesky, post-Berlin Wall world is looking at itself with despair over its confused societal values and personal emptiness. The church must translate these painful realities back to the world in terms of its insufficiency and inability to save itself. The church must proclaim anew the prophetic truth that it is not for humankind to find its own way.

Third, evangelism reaches its grand crescendo with its proclamation of *the all-sufficiency of Jesus Christ*. It is not enough simply to love, befriend, and serve unbelievers. It is not enough to lead them to a realization that their own worldviews and lifestyles are deficient. The moment comes when they must hear the gospel, confront the living Christ, and make a decision about his offer of pardon.

Sufficiency for the race's spiritual salvation is not found in the church. The church is composed of sinful-though-saved human beings who are trying to "live up to what we have already attained" (Phil. 3:16). A pilgrim church that has attained salvation by grace is still trying to live the implications of its status. Such a church is Christ's spiritual body, but it is inadequate to reflect the fullness of his holiness, love, and purity to the world. It is insufficient to do everything that needs to be done in his name in the world. And it is altogether insufficient to save anyone.

The church is "sufficient" for its evangelistic work only to the degree that it presents Jesus Christ to the world so he can draw people to himself for redemption. That is a very narrow and limited function for the church. The power to save is Christ's alone, and his faithful church discovers its insufficiency repeatedly and confesses his all-sufficiency with humility and joy.

Everything that is necessary to save anyone from the guilt, power, and eternal consequences of sin was done at the cross of Christ. The atonement is a finished work which is offered to sinners by grace. On his cross, Jesus suffered the spiritual separation from the Father (i.e., "My God, my God, why have you forsaken me!") which sinners were due to experience by virtue of our transgressions. Now, by virtue of divine mercy, sinners can stand before God in the righteousness of Jesus Christ by faith. "God made him who had no sin to be sin for us, so that in him we might become the righteousness of God" (2 Cor. 5:21).

Something over 4,000,000 people were Adolf Hitler's "guests" at Auschwitz between 1940 and 1945. Over your head even today as you pass through the gate of that camp are the German words *Arbeit macht frei!* In English, they mean "work liberates" or "work sets you free." It was a grotesque lie. Auschwitz was an end-of-the-line death camp where 2,000,000 Jews and 2,000,000 "undesirable" East Europeans died in a gas chamber, on the gallows, or in medical experiments. There was no mercy in the death camp. There was only work without reward. There was empty labor leading to earlier death. And there was false hope of freedom for those who believed a lie.

Yet how many people do we know who live by the same lie in their spiritual lives! Sensing their lostness and insufficiency, they have set about to be saved. They have put their hope in obeying enough "essential" commandments, attending enough of the "required" assemblies, and developing enough of the "necessary" Christian virtues to go to heaven. Such people feel no security about their salvation—and are absolutely mystified by those who do. "Duty" is the key noun in their theological vocabulary; "obey" is the operative verb. Yet they are never quite sure they have done their duty or obeyed enough of the right commands.

It is a scandalous and outrageous lie to teach that salvation arises from human activity of any sort. We do not contribute one whit to our salvation. *Arbeit macht frei!* is the falsehood against which both Romans and Galatians protest. "No one will be declared righteous in his sight by observing the law," said Paul (Rom. 3:20). By contrast, both Jews and Greeks "are justified freely by his grace through the redemption that came by Christ Jesus" (Rom. 3:24; cf. Gal. 3:10-14). Then there is his theological thunderbolt against it in Ephesians: "For it is by grace you have been saved, through faith—and this not from yourselves, it is the gift of God—not by works, so that no one can boast" (2:8-9).

Because God's standard can be nothing less than perfection, no amount of our correct theology, good deeds, charity, and piety can equal that requirement. Therefore anyone who is saved must renounce everything but the cross as his or her hope for eternal life. Anyone who tries to come to God by good works will miss the kingdom of God altogether. Anyone in the kingdom by grace through faith will fall away if he reverts to depending on good works in order to remain saved (Gal. 5:4). Abundant good works are the fruit of salvation in a Christian's life, but the finished work of Christ at Calvary is the only act of merit in human redemption. Until we renounce everything but Christ, we are prisoners in a death camp, embracing a lie as our hope, and forfeiting life.

It is the church's responsibility to proclaim this Good News of salvation in Christ to the world. Until he comes to claim us to himself, the story of the cross and its meaning must be our constant theme.

Conclusion

The world's most urgent need is to see God caring enough about us in our confusion and lostness to come among us, take our frailties and sinfulness onto himself, and pay the price of our redemption from sin. A world that senses Christ's presence through his church and which feels its own inadequacy for anything eternal will be ready to see the cross and its meaning. The mission of the church in evangelism is to expedite that process by preaching the gospel to every creature.

Ecclesiology
and
Eschatology

CHAPTER TEN

Baptism and Lord's Supper: Symbols of the Promise

Two of the continuing marks of the church through all its history are the central rites of baptism and the Lord's Supper. Though Christianity has been beset by divisions over how these acts are to be understood and administered, almost everyone agrees they are crucial to the ongoing life of the church. We are convinced that these are instances where theological principles are so enmeshed with their forms that a rejection of the forms entails significant theological loss. It may seem strange to see them included in the section of this book that points to an eschatological motif, but they uniquely bind together the past, present, and future of the church. To show their enduring significance is the goal of this chapter.

Baptism

One of the most crucial passages on the importance of baptism for the church is from what is probably Paul's earliest epistle: "You are all sons of God through faith in Christ Jesus, for all of you who were united with Christ in baptism have been clothed with Christ. There is neither Jew nor Greek, slave nor free, male nor female, for you are all one in Christ Jesus" (Gal. 3:26-28).

This passage claims that baptism is central to producing a unity in the body that obliterates the common barriers that are so much a part of the world. But how can this be? Again, it is Paul who provides a fundamental insight:

> What shall we say, then? Shall we go on sinning so that grace may increase? By no means! We died to sin; how can we live in it any longer? Or don't you know that all of us who were baptized into Christ Jesus were baptized into his death? We were therefore buried with him through baptism into death in order that, just as Christ was raised from the dead through the glory of the Father, we too may live a new life. . . . In the same way, count yourselves dead to sin but alive to God in Christ Jesus (Rom. 6:1-4, 11).

Baptism is the place where one dies. What is most crucial to Paul is not purification or even forgiveness, but death. The baptismal subject dies with Christ. That which finally breaks down the barriers of race, social status, and gender is death. Death is the great equalizer, the place where such distinctions truly make no difference.

Baptism initiates one into a communion in which the principle of entrance is the putting off of the self. There is no Jew or Greek, slave or free, male or female because these are all matters of differentiation that have no normative place when Christ lives in me.

Is there anyone among our readers who has not been part of an organization of some sort that has not had to struggle with the egos and self-seeking nature of its members? Here we begin to see clearly why baptism is so crucial to the life of the church. Only in a church of dead egos can these struggles cease. Only in a church composed of those who say "Not I, but Christ living in me" can we hope to have a body not torn by human ambition. The only hope for unity is not reformed character but dead egos.

But is this ever actually the case? Does baptism merely symbolize this, or is there some reality to it? In our assessment of baptism, we must chart a third course between the two extremes of merely symbolic interpretations and those that are crassly sacramental. On one reading, Paul himself struggled to navigate this alternate course:

> He by no means unconditionally attributes magic influence to baptism as if receiving it guaranteed salvation. . . . Nevertheless, baptism is an objective occurrence which happens to the baptized, not simply a symbol for a subjective process within him.[1]

In other words, while baptism does not work as some magic spell, neither is it just a symbol for a change of attitude the baptized one has exper-

---

1. Rudolph Bultmann, *Theology of the New Testament* (New York: Charles Scribner's Sons, 1955), I:312.

ienced. His or her relationship with God really changes in the event. In connection with the death of Christ, one experiences in a real, objective way becoming a "new creature." He stands justified before God, receives the Holy Spirit, and is empowered for righteous living. But will this new-creature status so change him that there will be no sign of the old self that has been dominated by selfish desire and willingness?

Perhaps the best way to address this question is by reference to Reinhold Niebuhr's description of the two aspects of God's grace. Grace is both forgiving and transforming. When either side is emphasized to the exclusion of the other, problems will surely follow.

When one emphasizes grace as forgiveness to the exclusion of grace as transformation, it will inevitably lead to sloppy living. There is no emphasis on becoming more like Christ, only on the forgiveness we constantly enjoy.

On the other hand, when all the weight of emphasis is placed on transformation to the exclusion of forgiveness, the result will likely be guilt-ridden neurosis. Since we constantly fall short of the call to be transformed into the image of God's own Son, a lack of proper attention to the forgiveness theme will quickly leave us overcome by our own inability.

Thus both must be emphasized. While God constantly forgives us, we expect to grow in righteousness and likeness to Christ. Baptism, properly understood, focuses on both. It is the point at which forgiveness finally becomes real, but it is only the beginning of the process of transformation. It is possible now to see why baptism has incontestable eschatological dimensions.

It is connected not just with Christ's death, but also his resurrection. As we noted in earlier chapters, the resurrection motif always has eschatological dimensions. While it is a past event, it is always pregnant with future promise.

First, we experience a true death to sin and self; these two factors will never again be the dominant forces in our lives. "But thanks be to God that, though you used to be slaves to sin, you wholeheartedly obeyed the form of teaching to which you were committed. You have been set free from sin and have become slaves to righteousness" (Rom. 6: 17-18).

Second, we also experience true transformation as a gift of God. "Therefore, if anyone is in Christ, he is a new creation; the old has gone, the new has come! All this is from God, who reconciled us to himself through Christ and gave us the ministry of reconciliation: that God was reconciling the world to himself in Christ" (2 Cor. 5:17-19a).

One should note in passing that the emphasis of this passage is on the work of God in baptism, not the action of the human being. Baptism is not portrayed in Scripture as a work one does. Baptism is more something done *to* the subject than *by* him. Thus the focus of a baptismal scene is not what the subject does but what the passive subject has done to him or her by God. This passivity of the subject is no accidental feature of baptism but is central to the ritual. Baptism is not self-administered but involves surrendering to another's power over him.

Just as one's body is given over to another and put in peril under the water, so one's life is being handed over to God and put at whatever risk is necessary for doing the divine will from now on.

This process of dying to self certainly does not end at baptism. What is initiated in this brief ceremony takes the remainder of life to finish. The Lord himself pointed out that taking up the cross was a daily process. So at baptism we are initiated into a spiritual reality that will reach its crescendo only at the end of time. Some Pauline scholars have described the life pursuant to baptism as "becoming what you are." You are a child of God by faith, so now you attempt to become that child in the way you live. You are dead to sin, so you now try to become dead to sin in your daily routine. You are dead to self, so now you try to become a person unencumbered by pride or ego.

Baptism is God's means of calling us into this experience and empowering us for the battle. It is the symbol of God's promise that what he has started in our lives and in our churches he will complete: the old passes away, and all things are made new!

The Lord's Supper

The Lord's Supper, like a many-faceted diamond, gives off different reflections depending on the angle from which one looks. It is communion, or it is Eucharist (i.e., Thanksgiving), or it is memorial. It is a powerful symbol, but it is also a divine reality. We wish to point out three aspects of the Lord's Supper that have special significance for the church as it anticipates a glorious future. These three aspects are (1) the Lord's Supper as an act of unity, (2) the Lord's Supper as the linking of past, present, and future, and (3) the Lord's Supper as proclamation of the gospel.

The Lord's Supper as an Act of Unity

Probably no passage in the New Testament points out the importance of the Lord's Supper for the continuing life of the church better than 1 Corinthians 11:17-33. Within this context, three verses in particular suggest the problems Paul was forced to address with this troubled church.

> When you come together, it is not the Lord's Supper you eat, for as you eat, each of you goes ahead without waiting for anybody else. One remains hungry, another gets drunk. Don't you have homes to eat and drink in? Or do you despise the church of God and humiliate those who have nothing? What shall I say to you? Shall I praise you for this? Certainly not! (1 Cor. 11:20-22).

Paul had earlier said (v. 17) one of the harshest things that could be uttered against a church: their meetings actually produced more harm than good. How was that happening? Apparently the church would assemble in the homes of its wealthier members, and during the agape feast (which was basically a fellowship meal), they would all partake of the Lord's Supper. Certain abuses had crept into the observance.

The Lord's Supper had become particularly divisive along socioeconomic lines in the church. The rich Christians who would supply the elements for the Lord's Supper, as well as the meal, were using the occasion to flaunt their superior economic status. They apparently would start earlier—a slave would not, of course, be free to leave his post early—and eat more and better food. Differences in menu is a time-honored way of pointing out one's superior position. It was in the midst of this situation that the Lord's Supper was eaten.

Paul points out that the mere performance of the act is no guarantee of a blessing from God, as some sacramentalists might contend. In fact, rather than being healing and re-creative, the Lord's Supper can actually become a source of judgment and death: "For anyone who eats and drinks without recognizing the body of the Lord eats and drinks judgment on himself. That is why many among you are weak and sick, and a number of you have fallen asleep" (1 Cor. 11:29-30).

The Lord's Supper was clearly intended to be a symbol of unity. "Because there is one loaf, we, who are many, are one body, for we all partake of the loaf" (1 Cor. 10:17). Paul contends that when one engages in this rite without proper regard for the body of Christ (i.e., fellow Christians) of which he or she is a part, nothing good can come of it. We take this to be the real import of verse 29 quoted above, where commentators admittedly differ on what "recognizing the body of the Lord" means. But no matter the interpretation given to this verse, the often-overlooked verse 33 points out the importance of "other-regard" in the participation of the Lord's Supper: "So then, my brothers, when you come together to eat, wait for each other."

The total passage is an important reminder that there are crucial and undeniable social factors involved in the Lord's Supper. It is not a private act of piety but a rite that has its proper place in community. Its simple but profound symbolism establishes a focus and rallying point for the church. In partaking of the body, the church becomes one body. It is that special time when the two incarnations come together symbolically—body to body. If the church ever comes to understand fully the depth of this mystery, then many of the petty divisions which plague it will cease. Power will replace routine, and the lordship of Christ will be truly proclaimed by the church—until the time the Lord proclaims it himself and when every tongue shall confess Jesus as Lord.

But what is symbolized here does not come to ultimate fruition before his appearing and kingdom. That is why this act is always eschatological. The supper calls the church to a unity that cannot be fully achieved, but for which we strive even now. Our fellowship is not based on commonalities of gender, status, or race but on our common salvation by the Lord who now reigns over us.

The Lord's Supper is a sobering reminder to every fractured church: there must be room for all at this fellowship. The Lord's Supper is an open invitation.

In our churches the Lord's Supper has long been separated from its original setting—the fellowship meal. In our formal worship settings, there is a great tendency to perceive this ritual as a personal transaction between an individual participant and God. But we dare not allow this to occur.

It is a proclamation of the new community, and therein lies an anticipation of the perfect heavenly fellowship. It is a symbol of the promise that, as God through Christ has called a people out from the world unto himself, he will complete the work he has started. There will be a kingdom where worldly distinctions cease and spiritual fellowship holds sway. We see it in the supper and in the promise of the future.

The Lord's Supper as Focus of Past, Present, and Future

It is absolutely crucial to note the dialectic between past and future in Paul's dealing with the words of institution:

> "This is my body, which is for you; do this in remembrance of me." In the same way, after supper he took the cup, saying, "This cup is the new covenant in my blood; do this, whenever you drink it, in remembrance of me." For whenever you eat this bread and drink this cup, you proclaim the Lord's death until he comes (1 Cor. 11:24-26).

The Lord's Supper is not merely a memorial, in the sense of simply remembering some past event. Like Passover, the past event being recalled continues to have impact in the present and projects us into the future.

Consider the Jews celebrating Passover long after they had comfortably settled in the Promised Land or the contemporary Jew observing Passover in his Manhattan apartment. Why relive the symbolism of eating the bitter herbs or assembling with staff in hand and ready to travel, though you have no place to go? It is the crucial point of connection between every Jew of all ages past, present, and future. The exodus is the act that gives identity to all Jews. The God they worship today is the God who delivered them from Egyptian bondage. It is more than an historical event. It is the point of religious identity.

The same is true of the Lord's Supper for Christians. It celebrates not just an event of history but the event that supplies every Christian throughout history with unique spiritual identity.

Just as devout Jews have lived between God's creation of the nation of Israel at the exodus and the anticipation of the coming reign of God in the Messiah, so Christians through the centuries live between the remembrance of the death of Christ and the anticipation of his return. It is what gives Christian history its continuity. While many things may change, the gospel does not.

The Lord's Supper as Proclamation

There is an old story about a father who ran off and left his wife and two children on Christmas eve. The family just couldn't believe it had really happened, so they decided to leave the Christmas tree up until the father came home. Months came and went. Eventually years went by, but still the tree was left in place. To take down the tree meant to give up all hope of his return. The tree became the symbol of that family's anticipation.

Just as the Christmas tree served as a continuing proclamation of one family's hope, the Lord's Supper is the constant proclamation of the Christian's expectation. When we cease to believe, we cease to participate in the Lord's Supper. It is our way of both telling the world and sharing with each other our continuing conviction of the power of the death of Christ.

One should note again here the anti-sacramental tone of the passage in 1 Corinthians. The mere observance of the act brings no compulsory blessing. In fact, one can come away from participation in the ritual worse off than when he went into it. The Lord's Supper certainly has the capacity to be a rich spiritual blessing from God, but it is not a magic potion at the disposal of the dispenser or partaker. Only when one approaches it with humility and hope, with love for brethren and love for God, does it work its power of God's grace. But, as Bonhoeffer points out, when this is the case it is as close to God's dream as the pilgrim church ever comes.

The day of the Lord's Supper is an occasion of joy for the Christian community. Reconciled in their hearts with God and the brethren, the congregation receives the gift of the body and blood of Jesus Christ, and, receiving that, it receives forgiveness, new life, and salvation. It is given new fellowship with God and men. The fellowship of the Lord's Supper is the superlative fulfillment of Christian fellowship. As the members of the congregation are united in body and blood at the table of the Lord so will they be together in eternity. Here the community has reached its goal. Here joy in Christ and his community is complete. The life of Christians together under the Word has reached its perfection in the sacrament.[2]

Symbols of the Promise

We close with a few reflections on the sense in which baptism and the Lord's Supper are truly "symbols of the promise." To do so, we must begin with some understanding of the difference in a symbol and a sign.

A sign is a pointer to some reality beyond itself. A symbol somehow actually participates in that reality. Perhaps an illustration will help clarify the matter. If you drive up to a street corner and see that someone has run over and mangled the stop sign, it generally creates no special feelings. How do you feel, on the other hand, when you see an American flag burning? The former is merely a sign, but the latter is a symbol. In a way that is impossible to explain fully, a country's flag participates in that for which it stands.

The same thing is uniquely true of both baptism and the Lord's Supper. They are symbols to be sure, but they are not just signs. As symbols, baptism and the Lord's Supper draw us in and make us participants in the death and resurrection of Christ. They make us a part of the 2000-year-old

---

2. Bonhoeffer, *Life Together*, p. 122.

Christian fellowship. They are constants in the life of the church because they allow participation in the heart of the gospel in a way that listening to preaching never can.

If someone decided to alter the shape or color of stop signs, we might find it inconvenient but not really threatening. If someone wished to alter the American flag, however, most people would be outraged because we identify with it so closely. While many things may change in the history of the church, baptism and the Lord's Supper must not. They are the constant symbols of the gospel proclaimed and the consummation anticipated. They are symbols of the promise of Jesus that remind us throughout all history:

> Do not let your hearts be troubled. Trust in God; trust also in me. There are many rooms in my Father's house; otherwise, I would have told you. I am going there to prepare a place for you. And if I go and prepare a place for you, I will come back and take you to be with me that you also may be where I am (John 14: 1-3).

Conclusion

As we close this chapter, we cannot help but note how ironical it is that two rites intended to be symbols and sources for unity have so often become points of contention and sources for division. Perhaps this points out more clearly than anything else what a chasm typically stretches between the two incarnations of the blessed Christ.

CHAPTER ELEVEN

The End of Time: The Glorified Church

The pilgrim church, whose challenges and struggles have been discussed in this book, will someday be a church at rest. God has not consigned the body of Christ to perpetual, chaotic motion without a goal. To the contrary, the biblical view of history is linear rather than cyclical. That is, the experience of God's people is not mere repetition of what has gone before and will happen again; we have a destination that has been set and identified for us by our Lord.

Before focusing on the church's future, we must admit a tension in its present status as a second incarnation. This tension has to do with a perspective and line of vision. Does the church discover its identity and find its mission via a backward-looking gaze? Or do we live and function as a forward-looking people?

Our answer to both questions is "Yes"—with a stipulation. Since Christ is the church's paradigm,

225

we will always look backward to his example and
teaching. That much has been made clear from the
beginning of this volume. We also look back to the
experiences of the various churches whose accomplishments and failures are chronicled in Acts. We
continue to read the epistolary counsel given to
those churches. While rooted in the past, however,
the church's passion must always be directed to the
future. Christianity which is true to its origins will
always be eschatological (i.e., concerned with final
and ultimate things) in its essence.

What is the theme of the assorted kingdom parables recorded in Matthew 13? A sower scatters seed
with a view toward harvesting 30, 60, or 100 times
what was sown, not simply to keep himself busy or
to create a memory (vv. 3-23). Weeds sown by an
enemy with another farmer's wheat are allowed to
grow with the grain—until the harvest (vv. 24-30).
The tiny mustard seed grows into the largest of garden plants over a period of time (vv. 31-32). Yeast
works through a great lump of dough when given
time (v. 33). Treasure discovered in a field (v. 44) or a
valuable pearl located by a merchant (v. 45) doesn't
simply establish a vivid memory; it determines activity in the direction of a future goal of ownership.
A net cast into a lake catches all kinds of fish and
requires a separation after the net has been pulled
to the shore (vv. 47-50).

Chapter Four of this book delineated the nature
of the church as a kingdom-seeking body. The
fruition of that search comes at the end, not at the
beginning. The parables of Matthew 13 verify that
thesis. True enough, we have been "rescued from

the dominion of darkness" and transplanted into the "kingdom of the Son" (Col. 1:13), but the fullness of the kingdom experience lies ahead.

Perhaps it is helpful to draw a parallel with eternal life, redemption, and salvation. Each of these is both a present possession and a future prospect. Believers in Christ have been made alive with him and saved by his grace (Eph. 2:5, 8); salvation is therefore ours now. Yet the fact remains that salvation is also presented as something belonging to the time of Christ's return. He will "appear a second time" and will do so "to bring salvation to those who are waiting for him" (Heb. 9:28). Thus it seems clear from the biblical text that salvation can be viewed as both a present and future possession; it is already present in terms of our deliverance from the guilt and dominion of sin, but it is not yet present in its fullness of deliverance from all things that could hinder faithfulness. This already-but-not-yet understanding of salvation makes it possible to interpret this statement from Paul: "Our salvation is nearer now than when we first believed" (Rom. 13:11). Weren't these Christians at Rome saved when they accepted Jesus? Yes, but the finality of their salvation would be realized only at "his appearing and his kingdom" (cf. 2 Tim. 4:1).

Looking to "The End"

The biblical view of history has an end in view. But it is an end that is understood as a goal, not simply a terminus. While watching a boring movie, "The End" signifies cessation. The final scene may

have been garbled. The plot may not have reached
a conspicuous or satisfactory resolution. Welcome
as the end may be in such a setting, it is ambiguous and unsatisfying. Not so when Scripture
speaks of the end of things.

"For as in Adam all die, so in Christ all will be
made alive. . . . Then the end will come, when he
hands over the kingdom to God the Father after he
has destroyed all dominion, authority and power"
(1 Cor. 15:22, 24). This is an "end" to things in
terms of their destination, goal, and proper outcome.
When Christ has subjected all things to the divine
will forever, God will be "all in all" (1 Cor. 15:28).
Cessation or intention? "And [God] made known to
us the mystery of his will according to his good pleasure, which he purposed in Christ, to be put into effect when the times will have reached their fulfillment—to bring all things in heaven and on earth
together under one head, even Christ" (Eph. 1:9-10).

Ah, there it is! The unfolding of human history
is not cyclical, pointless, and vain. Nor is history,
as Voltaire once wrote, "nothing but a pack of tricks
that we play upon the dead." God's purpose is being
worked out in the arena of our tumult. He is bringing sons and daughters to glory. He is acting to
unite our fragmented world in the Son. He desires
our salvation and waits to give us a "rich welcome
into the eternal kingdom of our Lord and Savior
Jesus Christ" (2 Pet. 1:11).

Where, then, shall we build our hopes? Most
people who have ever lived seem to have assumed a
sort of limitlessness to this life. They have pushed
away the truth of life's brevity and uncertainty.

Thus they have seen no urgency to an existence they have viewed as open-ended. But those who have taken Jesus seriously have sensed the need to build for a world yet to come.

Christians have echoed the aphorism of Jesus about gaining the whole world yet forfeiting our souls. They have told and retold his story about the Rich Man and Lazarus, saying that one's status in this world is not a sure index to his or her future prospects. They have talked about readiness for the return of Christ and heralded his parousia. Awaiting that coming and presence, they have been busy trying to fulfill their master's wishes in his absence. Anticipation of his appearing and kingdom has given the church direction during its pilgrimage.

"May God himself, the God of peace, sanctify you through and through. May your whole spirit, soul and body be kept blameless at the coming of our Lord Jesus Christ. The one who calls you is faithful and he will do it" (1 Thess. 5:23). "Dear friends, now we are children of God, and what we will be has not yet been made known. But we know that when he appears, we shall be like him, for we shall see him as he is. Everyone who has this hope in him purifies himself, just as he is pure" (1 John 3:2-3). "In all my prayers for all of you, I always pray with joy because of your partnership in the gospel from the first day until now, being confident of this, that he who began a good work in you will carry it on to completion until the day of Christ Jesus" (Phil. 1:4-6).

Linking "Already" and "Not Yet"

The texts just cited affirm that a future glorification is the church's destiny. They also assume that the knowledge of such a fate will make a difference in the present. The theological term that summarizes everything involved in this affirmation and assumption is hope.

Don't unbelievers dismiss this orientation to the future as just so much "pie in the sky by and by"? What can we say to their negative critique of what we affirm positively as our "blessed hope—the glorious appearing of our great God and Savior, Jesus Christ"? (cf. Tit. 2:13).

Karl Marx chided the notion of eternity, heaven, and prospects beyond this life as distractions. On his limited view of things, all these were fantasies employed by weak people to ease their pain and played upon by their oppressors to keep them from taking up arms to change the world. As a thoroughgoing materialist, he pleaded that such a mythical view of things be rejected in favor of a commitment to the here-and-now world of the five senses.

Marx was wrong. Believing in eternal realities does not diminish the importance of life now; to the contrary, it magnifies the significance of the present. Faith is not a coward's way of coping with unpleasant realities; it is the basis for courage in tackling them. It is not a means for the church to escape responsibility to the world; faith in things that lie ahead is its justification for shouldering its duty to social justice, compassion, and good deeds.

If everything ends at the cemetery, there is no ultimate meaning to anything in your life. You have no responsibility to anyone but yourself. Trying to change anything about our world would be the pinnacle of arrogance, for there would be no way of knowing that your vision of a better world was any better than that of your arch-enemy.

If Jesus is coming back, however, your life does have meaning. Your freedom to make decisions is significant, for permanent consequences follow from those decisions. Morality is real. Love will conquer hatred. Good will triumph over evil. And between the "already" of a salvation received on the basis of Christ's redemptive mission and the "not yet" of his eternal kingdom, the church has important things to do. Because of a divine dominion already witnessed in Jesus as our exemplar, we participate in the kingdom of heaven and await with confidence the full realization of all his reign entails.

Thus it is that the church's eschatological prospects make its current activities important. God-directed worship not only creates an intense present experience of encounter with him but evokes a longing for the time when we will know him fully. The Lord's Supper not only reminds us of the cross and empty tomb but functions continually as a forward-looking proclamation of the Lord's death until he comes. The believing community finds justification for facing and dealing with difficulties—even persecution—for the sake of what lies ahead. Caring about others, telling the truth, being involved with this world to improve it, mak-

ing it aware of its destiny, sharing the message of
the cross—all these are compelled by an expectation of his return.

Remembering that everything about the church
must pass the "Jesus test" to be trustworthy, it is
easy to show the eschatological goal of his life and
ministry. "And now, Father," he prayed on the eve
of his death, "glorify me in your presence with the
glory I had with you before the world began" (John
17:5). How resolute this goal made him in hard-
ship—and the implications of that for us—is clear
from this encouragement: "Let us fix our eyes on
Jesus, the Pioneer and Perfecter of our faith, who
for the joy set before him endured the cross, scorn-
ing its shame, and sat down at the right hand of
the throne of God. Consider him who endured such
opposition from sinful men, so that you will not
grow weary and lose heart" (Heb. 12:2-3).

Jesus identified with the poor, sick, excluded,
and sinful. He washed feet, touched lepers, and
cuddled children. He suffered from misunder-
standing, intolerance, and acrimony. He chose to
submit to the humiliation of the cross. And all this
was for the sake of "the joy set before him."

Since Jesus prayed for his disciples "to be with
me where I am and to see my glory" (John 17:24),
we must assume that he wants us to follow his
path of humility, service, willingness to suffer, and
even death and to find motivation for our pilgrim-
status where he found encouragement during his
own. Look to the end. Know the outcome. Keep all
things in perspective against the goal.

Hope is the Guiding Star for a pilgrim church that is seeking the fullness of the kingdom. "Hope that is seen is no hope at all," said Paul. "Who hopes for what he already has? But if we hope for what we do not yet have, we wait for it patiently" (Rom. 8:24b-25).

We already hold shares in the kingdom of heaven, but the fullness of that kingdom has not come. Sometimes there is frustration in our wait, but there is also anticipation, excitement, and motivation. For the sake of those around us, we want to introduce whatever we can of the knowledge of Christ into our environment. But if the world rejects both him and us, we take comfort in the knowledge that this world does not have the final say. It is passing away. When the new heaven and new earth have come, we will know Christ better than we can possibly experience him now.

From the perspective of the end, today's struggles will only add zest to the triumph. Maternity wings in hospitals, after all, are not gloomy places. There is pain in giving birth. Tears are shed. There are even screams. But those things give way to the euphoria of birth. "We know that the whole creation has been groaning as in the pains of childbirth, right up to the present time. Not only so, but we ourselves, who have the firstfruits of the Spirit, groan inwardly as we wait eagerly for our adoption as sons, the redemption of our bodies. For in this hope we were saved" (Rom. 8:22-24a).

Conclusion

Mingled with our certainty in his coming is an acknowledged uncertainty about the time of his coming. Thus the church awaits its Savior with both poise and anticipation, with both assurance and suspense. Avoiding the trap of trying to fix the time of an event once kept from both angels and the Son (Matt. 24:36), we simply know that his return is drawing nearer every day.

When he appears, we will be like him. When he returns, the kingdom will arrive in its fullness. When the bridegroom appears, the attendants who have waited through the night will rejoice. The pains of labor will give way to the delight of birth. The farmer's patience will be justified by the harvest. "I consider that our present sufferings are not worth comparing to the glory that will be revealed in us" (Rom. 8:18).

The church of Jesus Christ does not float in what one writer has called an "existential present." It has a known and definitive past; it has a certain and desirable future. And those end-time prospects of sharing in Christ's glory are drawing nearer as we enter the 21st century. Our task while waiting is not to bring them to fruition but to be a responsive and healthy body to our head.

Far from being pie in the sky, our expectation of sharing Christ's glory is at the heart of our faith. It is not dessert but part of the main course. For the church cannot be faithful as a second incarnation without the boldness that comes of certainty in the very great and precious promises made to it by Christ.

The 21st-century church looks beyond its own situation in space and time to a destiny pledged by its head, Jesus Christ. With its future assured, it can find the motivation to face its current challenges with boldness.

Conclusion

Summing Up and Looking Ahead

At the end of a book such as *The Second Incarnation*, two questions must be asked. If they cannot be answered, all the words on all the pages have been only an exercise in futility. Its authors may have filled their time and indulged their imaginations, but they have done nothing of real value. Against the dictum that theology cannot be practical, we believe the issues explored in this book can and must lead to church renewal in the 21st century.

The two questions staring us in the face are these: (1) What has been said? (2) What difference is made if anybody has heard it?

Question One must be answered in terms of a brief summary of the eleven chapters you have read. Without going to the trouble of walking back through the chapters one by one, it must be enough here to offer that *The Second Incarnation* has said that the church must break out of its traditional ways of seeing itself for the sake of spiritual vitality in the new century. Those of us who are insiders to the church have fallen into the rut of perpetuating fallible—even corrupt and toxic—theologies, projects, and systems. We have become too defensive of the status quo. This book has argued for a fresh look at the biblical model of the church as the body of Christ.

We have said that a major mistake of the church over the centuries has been "comparing ourselves with ourselves" (cf. 2 Cor. 10:12) rather than seeing Jesus alone as the paradigm for the church. Our goal is not to salvage and give back to the world the eighteenth-century, ninth-century, or first-century church. All those churches have been defective attempts by saved-but-still-sinful people to stand in for Jesus Christ in the world. Just as Hollywood uses stand-ins and "body doubles" for its stars, so the church is attempting to represent Christ within its environment. As God was incarnate a first time in him, so he seeks to be incarnate perpetually through the church that dares to wear his name.

Though never without a transcendent and trans-cultural dimension due to its critical place in God's eternal purpose, there is still no finality for the church at any point in history prior to Christ's appearing and kingdom. Humans know of and are the church within the narrow limits of our fallen cultures, insights, and traditions. It is therefore inappropriate for us to spend too much time inspecting each other—whether to boast of *our* "rightness" or to condemn *their* "wrongness." All are under the judgment of God that we are less than we were meant to be. Only by keeping our eyes on Christ as exemplar do we maintain the appropriate humility and find the suitable motivation for any of the things we do.

The church is less an institution to be created (or *re*-created) by us than a living organism. It alternately flourishes and wastes away, thrives with spiritual health and languishes with countless infirmities. It is the body of Christ in the world. It is that public entity charged by God to carry on in its corporate life what Jesus began to do and teach in his personal life.

This shifting of perspective has implications for everything about the church's life. It means that we need not fear change but expect it, for incremental change is the order of living things. Babies grow, trim waists thicken, failing eyesight calls for corrective lenses, and treatment brings sick persons back to health. All living bodies are constantly undergoing change. Only preserved corpses never alter in form and appearance.

Thus we have the right to reconsider our identity under the Pauline metaphor of the church as body of Christ and trace out some of the implications it has for us. Worship, life, mission, and evangelism all take on new appearances. We simultaneously have a healthier self-image and realize the need each of us in Christ has for every other. Denominational loyalties give way to Christ-centeredness, and what we have called "line-item theology" is replaced by Christological reading of Holy Scripture. We honor and preserve certain cherished traditions, but we preserve them *as traditions* without consciously or unconsciously elevating them to the status of dogma. We begin to experience freedom for our own unique spiritual adventures in Christ and, at the same time, feel the tendency to judge others in theirs dropping away.

Question Two has to be answered provisionally rather than authoritatively. If people took this biblical idea seriously, significant changes would certainly occur. We think those changes would be for the better and have tried to sketch the substance of those changes in the earlier chapters of this book. At the same time, we are practical enough to know that this shift of paradigm will be met by significant resistance. Some will misunderstand our point, and some will resist it because they comprehend it clearly and feel threatened by it.

We would like to think that people who embrace so noble and Christ-exalting a project could move ahead without either being castigated or feeling smug. From the history of ideas over the centuries, we know how unlikely that is. The status quo is never questioned without peril. The ones being questioned become defensive, mount an attack against the searchers, and try to discount those who have dared register their serious concerns by discrediting both their questions and their motivations. Giving too little credit to their forebears, the ones doing the questioning are sometimes tactless, come across as self-righteous, and do unnecessary harm. While these dangers are acknowledged, we still believe the alternative of perpetuating a theologically impoverished and practically deleterious ecclesiology is even worse.

An expert in the 21st-century phenomenon of computer technology has made the suggestion that since technical advances are moving so rapidly in that field, there need to be periodic cycles of house-cleaning.

> We computer types get trapped by technologies—often technologies from just one or two companies. To get out of these traps, we need to revive that time-honored Aztec custom of cyclical destruction and renewal. But we'd need a much smaller Sun Calendar because our "end-of-the-world" cycles should run five years, max.[1]

The Aztec custom he refers to was a destruction of their worldly goods on a regular schedule. They believed that the world would end after one 52-year cycle or another. Before their priests went off to await the potential end each time, they destroyed the worldly goods they had accumulated over the past 52 years.

One of the most interesting comments about this proposal to his colleagues was its author's admitted problem in finally taking it to heart in his own office. On the one hand, he began sorting hardware, software, books, and other items only to be "amazed at how unimportant all of that stuff had become." On the other hand, however, he conceded: "I was also struck by what I was and wasn't willing to throw out."[2]

---

1. Barry Gerber, "Something New Under the Sun," *Network Computing* (November 1991): 128.

2. Ibid.

Maybe some real-life variety of this approach needs to be incorporated into the modern church. While everything certainly does not need to be scrapped every five years, everything must be constantly reexamined. Surely we ought to be *willing* to scrap anything other than the gospel message itself to reach the lost and keep the saved. Traditional ways of doing things that no longer meet the needs of the people going through those motions need to be discarded. "We've never done it that way before" should be identified as a forbidden objection to any serious proposal for the church's methodology; each proposal must be weighed on its own merits for the task at hand of being Christ's presence in a given setting. We have seen it happen again and again. Someone will admit that a method of long standing is "not really working any more" or that a suggested alternative "isn't biblically wrong," but the old will not be changed and the new will not be adopted. A curious psychology thus stands in the way of better theology and more effective methodology. Changes in time-honored ways of doing things are difficult for *some* of us to accept even in theory and even harder still for *all* of us in practice.

What, then, would happen if these things were taken seriously? There could be healthy, creative, and liberating change. There would emerge the possibility of reaching millions of people whom we now impress only negatively, if at all. We could become a more attractive, robust, and resourceful body to our head, the Lord Jesus Christ. Like the computer whiz who eventually filled "one very large dumpster" with useless artifacts he was warehousing, we would likely have a tidier world from which to pursue God without pointless encumbrances.

What we attempt in trying to be the church is too grand for us. It is only by grace that we are called to such a role at all. For all our bungling and failing, though, we keep trying with bold assurance. With greater success on some days than on others, we persevere. But we do not give up.

Someday our Savior will appear, and the grace that has called us to this too-great-for-us task will finally complete his purpose in us by perfecting a too-wonderful-to-imagine redemption. *Come, Lord Jesus!*